WITHIN YOUR REACH

by Bill Hodges

60 POSITIVE MESSAGES FOR A MORE PRODUCTIVE LIFE

Editor
B. Phyllis Naylor

Cover Design
Jerry Presnell

©1989 William N. Hodges
Library of Congress # 89-84006
ISBN 0-9622717-0-5

Published by
Great Day Books

For information concerning Bill Hodges, his
column, books, or seminars, please write to:

Hodges Seminars
P.O. Box 22, Fairborn, OH 45324
513/878-9701

PREFACE

This book began as an idea in 1987. During a conversation with a newspaper editor, I made the off-hand comment that newspapers seemed to be overloaded with negative material. I went on to say that there should be a counterbalance—some small section of the paper dedicated to brightening the lives of the readers. That newspaper editor, Bob Gremling, turned the tables on me. He challenged me to look for something positive to say, and to do it on a regular basis. So was born our syndicated column "Posi–Talk." Contained within this book is a collection of columns I wrote for you.

You may wonder how I can write a column for you, especially if we have never met. The answer is that, whether we have met or not, I know a great deal about you. You see, as much I believe that each of us is unique, there is much that we have in common. We all want to be loved, we want to feel needed, we want to feel useful, and we want to feel that we have invested our lives rather than spent them. This book looks at our common problems and offers ideas that will help us to build upon our strengths and create a lifetime which will return dividends, not only to ourselves but to those around us.

Because we are unique, we move through life in different ways and at different speeds. An article that you read now may not meet an immediate need, because of where you are in your journey. I encourage you to read this book at least once a year. I believe that this will do several things. First, it will help you to maintain a positive mental attitude which will, in turn, allow you to approach any problem that you have as a stepping stone, rather than as a stumbling block. Second, because we do change and grow, we may be better prepared to understand or see a meaning for us in a particular article at a later date more clearly than we might now.

You will probably notice that every thought contained within these pages is NOT an original thought by Bill Hodges. I stand on the shoulders of giants. These columns also contain the wisdom of knowledgeable men and women from Socrates to Sachel Paige. Just as knowledge has no clear beginning and no end, so it is with this book. It is a collection of our ideas randomly presented, and I am the conduit through which they find their way to you.

You will read a number of times in these essays that you are unique, you are special, and you are great, but it is not until you begin to believe this for yourself that everything you want will be WITHIN YOUR REACH.

ABOUT THE AUTHOR

William N. "Bill" Hodges, DTM, is a man of many interests and accomplishments. He began his business career in the field of sales and marketing, and became at a very early age a top sales producer for two Fortune 500 companies. A developing interest in communications then led him into a variety of fields that helped him more clearly define his own lifetime goals—to reach personal success and satisfaction through helping others live more productive lives. Bill is president of Hodges Seminars, a firm that develops sales meetings, training programs, and educational seminars of all types. His programs are attended by personnel from many Fortune 500 companies, major associations, and government agencies in the United States and Canada.

Experienced in media, as well as live audience communications, Bill has hosted his own television interview/public affairs program and radio talk show. He has authored numerous articles, and has written for many business publications. The articles contained in this book are from his nationally syndicated newspaper column, "Positive Talk." Bill has discovered many positive ideas that, when put into practice, enable people to realize their most valued dreams. In this book, he relates them to you in an interesting and thoroughly absorbing way.

This book is dedicated to my wife, Judy, and to all the spouses who have ever worked together on a project.

TABLE OF CONTENTS

A GREAT THING HAPPENED ON THE DAY YOU WERE BORN.

THE WORLD WAS A NICER PLACE.

.X.

We hold these truths to be self—evident: that all men are created equal; that they are endowed by their Creator with certain inalienable rights; that among these are life, liberty, and the pursuit of happiness.

Thomas Jefferson "Declaration of Independence"

WITHIN YOUR REACH

If there is anything about these columns that I hope impacts upon the reader, it is that you were born to succeed. You were born to be happy, to be proud of yourself, and to have the respect of people around you. It is like having a legacy or birthright, and yet there is a price to be paid in order to receive it. You must be willing to believe in yourself and to reach out. Throughout the years, I have watched many people sit back as the world passed them by. They complained that everyone else seemed to get the breaks, and all they ever got was broken. For the most part, these people refused to reach out and take what was presented to them.

I remember the story of a man named Joe who was caught in a flood. As the water drew ever higher on his home, he climbed ever closer to the roof, finally ending up on the peak holding onto the chimney. A man in a rowboat came by and offered to take Joe from the roof, to which Joe replied, "No thank you, God will save me." A little while later, a larger boat came by and the skipper offered to rescue Joe from the roof. Again he said, "No thank you, God will save me." Finally, noting Joe's predicament, a Coast Guard helicopter swooped low over his home and offered him a line to safety. Once more he replied, "No thank you, God will save me." Shortly after the last offer of assistance, the waters finally rose high enough to wash Joe off the roof and he was drowned in the torrent. He ascended into heaven and stood before God. He looked at God and said, "You promised! You promised that you would always take care of me. How could you possibly let me drown?" God looked at Joe and in a soft voice replied, "I didn't let you drown, I sent you two boats and a helicopter. It was you who chose to drown!" God gave him the opportunities. It was Joe who chose not to take them.

The opportunity is there, all the time, for each of us to be happy. For most of us, it's simply a matter of getting started—to take the first step—to begin believing in ourselves and that we are worthy of having the good things in life. Joe expected a miracle but didn't recognize one when it appeared. Do you recognize the miracle that you are? There has never been nor will there ever be a person just like you. You are special! You are unique! You are great! You have much to offer the world. You were born with the right to expect good things to happen to you. You deserve love, friendship, respect, happiness, wealth, purpose, hope, direction, security, health, peace, and freedom.

It is up to you whether you claim your birthright. When you finally believe that you are worthy and you are willing to act on your belief, all of the riches in the universe are within your reach.

We ought not to say, what could I have been if I had started then, but rather what can I be if I start now.

W. N. Hodges

STARTING TODAY . . . .

As we travel around the country sharing ideas with various groups, audiences from 10 to 3,000 have had at least one common thread. When I tell them, "Raise your hand if you are a procrastinator," in every audience, slowly, over half the attendees raise their hands. If I asked you that same question, would you raise your hand? If so, these ideas offered by Gerald B. Klein will be of value to you:

Today is here. I will start with a smile and resolve to be agreeable. I will not criticize. I will refuse to waste my valuable time.

Today . . in one thing I know I am equal with all others . . time. All of us draw the same salary in seconds, minutes, and hours.

Today I will not waste my time because the minutes I wasted yesterday are as lost as a vanished thought.

Today I refuse to spend time worrying about what might happen . . . it usually doesn't. I am going to spend time making things happen.

Today I am determined to study to improve myself, for tomorrow I may be wanted, and I must not be found lacking.

Today I am determined to do the things I should do. I firmly determine to stop doing the things I should not do.

Today I begin by doing and not wasting my time. In one week I will be miles beyond the person I am today.

Today I will not imagine what I would do if things were different. They are not different. I will make success with what material I have.

Today I will stop saying, "If I had time . . . " I know I never will find time for anything. If I want time, I must make it.

Today I will act toward other people as though this might be my last day on earth. I will not wait for tomorrow. Tomorrow never comes.

The inability to effectively manage our lives has a marked effect on how we feel about ourselves. The first step in attaining a positive mental attitude is to attain a good feeling about ourselves. Let's start today to take control of our own life. The longest journey begins with the first step. Don't be afraid to take that step.

The first requisite of a good citizen in this Republic of ours is that he shall be able and willing to pull his weight.

Theodore Roosevelt

THE PRICE OF MEMBERSHIP

This time of year, I, like many people, begin to complain about the taxes I have to pay. This year I made a very bad mistake. I complained to my friend Hugo. Hugo looked at me with a very serious face and said, "Considering the initiation fee I had to pay, the dues are cheap." I asked Hugo what he meant about paying an initiation fee, and dues to what? His reply started me thinking. He said that back in the 50's when he came to this country, his native land of Hungary was in a state of war. In order to come to the United States, he and his family had to crawl through the mud, under the barbed wire, while trying to avoid the watchful eyes of the armed sentries. To Hugo, this was the initiation fee he and his family paid to join the greatest club in the world, and taxes are the dues he pays to keep it strong.

Hugo's comments caused me to think of a friend I have in Florida named Peppi. Peppi told me that in order to get an exit visa he had to work in a Cuban cane field for two years without pay. At the end of two years, the Cuban government confiscated all of his belongings. He and his family were allowed to take only the clothes on their backs when they left Cuba to come to Miami. This was Peppi's initiation fee. Since that time, Peppi and his wife have raised two lovely daughters, each of whom have a college education, and Peppi has become a foreman at a boat company. Peppi doesn't think the dues are high.

My own family came to this great country from Canada, and our initiation fee was a $1 trip across the Ambassador Bridge. That's not much of a fee compared to that paid by Hugo and Peppi. Maybe it's the low initiation fee most of us paid and the ease with which we joined this club that has caused us to lose sight of its great value.

You can bet that around the world there are hundreds of potential members who would willingly pay any price to take our place. They're confined by brick walls in East Germany, and behind iron and bamboo curtains in other parts of the world. This year on April 15, when we send in our taxes, instead of frowning, let's try and remember the people like Hugo and Peppi and the initiation fee they had to pay. When you think about it, the dues aren't high to belong to the most sought after club in the world. For those dues, you can say, "I AM AN AMERICAN."

We are made strong by what we overcome.
John Burroughs

IT CAN'T BE DONE, OR CAN IT?

Over the years I have been blessed with the opportunity to meet a number of people who, by any sense of the word, would be considered successful. One such man was Bill Lear. I was only eighteen when I met Mr. Lear, and at that tender age I was in awe of this master inventor. After all, he had taken on the giants and had done the things that people said could not be done. With the naivete of youth, I asked him for his secret of success. He reached into his drawer and withdrew a piece of paper on which he said was contained the secret to success. Written on that paper were these words by Edgar A. Guest:

IT COULDN'T BE DONE

Somebody said that it couldn't be done,
But he with a chuckle replied
That maybe it couldn't,
But he would be one who wouldn't say so 'til he'd tried.
So he buckled right in
With the trace of a grin on his face.
If he worried, he hid it.
He started to sing as he tackled the thing
That couldn't be done, and he did it.

Somebody scoffed: "Oh, you'll never do that,
At least no one ever has done it."
But he took off his coat and he took off his hat,

And the first thing we knew he'd begun it.
With a lift of his chin and a bit of a grin,
Without any doubting or quiddit.
He started to sing as he tackled the thing
That couldn't be done and he did it.

There are thousands to tell you it cannot be done,
There are thousands to prophesy failure.
There are thousands to point out to you,
One by one, the dangers that wait to assail you.
But just buckle in with a bit of a grin,
Just take off your coat and go to it.
Just start to sing as you tackle the thing,
That cannot be done and you'll do it.

I've read this poem many times and have been reminded of Mr. Lear's "I can" philosophy. As a result, I have found the courage to tackle problems and to grasp opportunities that seemed beyond me. Some were beyond me, but most were not, and the same will be true in your life. The next time someone says to you, "It cannot be done," simply smile and then DO IT!!

Life shrinks or expands in proportion to one's courage.

Anais Nin

THANK GOD, MY HANDICAPS DON'T SHOW

On a cold snowy day just before Christmas, I drove up to the Kroger store to get a few items. The parking lot was full, except for those few spots right up front marked "Handicapped." I remember thinking, "I won't be here long, and it's a long walk from the back of the parking lot." But then I thought, "No, those are for handicapped people. Thank God, I'm not handicapped."

As I walked from the back of the lot, a sports car passed me and pulled right into a handicapped spot. Feelings of anger bubbled up inside of me, until I noticed that the driver had reached into the back seat of his car, pulled out a wheelchair and then proceeded to lower himself into it. Again I said to myself, "Thank God, I'm not handicapped."

Both the young man and I checked out at the same time. As I watched him reach up with difficulty to pay for his purchases, I again said to myself, "Thank God, I'm not handicapped." As we left the store, he noticed an older woman carrying a heavy package. He tugged on her sleeve and suggested that if she would put the package in his lap, he would wheel it out to the car for her. He thought to help. I didn't. This time I thought, "Thank God, my handicaps don't show."

I've come to believe that it's not what we don't have that causes us to be handicapped, but rather what we don't do with what we do have. Both he and I had the same opportunity to be of service. He used what he had to advantage. I saw the wheelchair as a shackle but he saw it as a tool to be used. I don't know the young man, but even though he's minus two legs, I doubt that he considers himself handicapped. I certainly don't.

It is easy for us, even comfortable, to blame our lack of success on real or imagined handicaps. Yet handicapped people have been very successful. Beethoven created some of the world's greatest music even after he became too deaf to carry on a conversation. Grandma Moses, who could no longer do needlework because her hands were crippled by arthritis, went on to become a great primitive painter. Stevie Wonder, who was born blind, brightens the world with his music. You see, it's not the handicap, but rather how we let the handicap affect us, that tells us how far we can go.

Habit with him was all the test of truth, "It must be right: I've done it from my youth."
George Crabbe

THE SILKEN CORD

Once upon a time, a maharajah was given a beautiful black leopard cub. The maharajah wanted to be able to keep the cub with him and to walk down the street with it. How though, could he hold back such a powerful beast, once it grew older. He went to his wise men with the problem. They advised him to put a very heavy rope around the young cat's neck, one so strong that no matter how hard the cub pulled, the cub could not possibly break the rope.

The cub soon learned that the feel of the collar around its neck and the slight tug of the rope represented the boundaries to which it could go. Little by little, the cub gave up its free will and became a slave to the rope. Then day by day, the size of the rope was diminished until all that was left was a silken cord.

All who saw the maharajah walk the leopard on the silken tether knew immediately that the leopard, with little effort, could snap the cord and run free. Everyone knew he could break free except the leopard. For it really wasn't the silken cord that held him, but rather the heavy ropes in his mind. Many of us are like the leopard.

All of us are bound by the silken cords of past conditioning. We try to be free, but each time we try, we feel cords from the past tugging at us. The cords caused by conditioning words such as: "A woman's place is in the home." "Men don't hug men." "What will the neighbors think?" "Clean your plate. Children in China are starving." In my own case, even though I know there's no logical relationship between cleaning my plate and children starving in China, I still can't leave food on my plate without a feeling of guilt.

Cords woven by past conditioning can be broken and we can be free. The first step toward freedom is to believe that they can be broken. The second is to begin questioning their value and validity. The third is to have faith in our own judgement. And last, we must move toward independent action. That action may include what WE deem valid from the past, but it must meet today's needs and be reasonable for our future well–being. It's always up to us. We can dare to be free or we can live our lives restricted by the silken cord.

Man's happiness in life is the result of man's own effort and is neither the gift of God nor a spontaneous natural product.

Ch'en Tu–hsiu

HAVE A NICE DAY?

Over the past few years, it has become common practice by many warm and sunny people to express the greeting to others, "Have a nice day." It does make you feel good when someone smiles and utters these words. But do people really just "have" nice days? Some do, but is it really worth the gamble to leave it to chance? I can't guarantee you a nice day, but if you will practice these ten suggestions, you may be able to <u>make</u> it a nice day.

1. When you wake up in the morning, think of something nice that you can do for someone else during the day.

2. Give each person in your house a smile, a hug and an "I love you." If you live alone and have a dog, take a minute to pat the dog.

3. On your drive to work, resolve to smile at those who cut in front of you. Relax at the stoplights and listen to music.

4. Whatever the weather, make it work for you. Enjoy the sunny days, and remember that the rainy days bring the beautiful flowers.

5. Tackle the toughest problems first, while your mind is alert.

6. Stay away from sugary snacks at coffee breaks, and eat a light lunch. Remember, we are what we eat, and some of us are dangerously close to being a jelly donut.

7. Appreciate the work of people around you. Take every opportunity to tell someone they've done a good job.

8. Take pride in the work you do, no matter what your position.

9. Take responsibility for yourself and your own actions.

10. Associate with positive people, repeating only that gossip which reflects well on others.

In a song by John Denver is the line, "Some days are diamonds, and some days are stones." The diamond days are a gift. It's what we make of the stones that will shape our lives. Next time someone says, "Have a nice day," smile and think to yourself, "I'll make it a nice day."

Gossip is mischievous, light and easy to raise, but grievous to bear and hard to get rid of. No gossip ever dies away entirely, if many people voice it: it too is a kind of divinity.

Hesiod

STICKS AND STONES . . .

Remember when we chanted the rhyme as children, "Sticks and stones will break my bones, but words will never hurt me"? Many of us have long since healed up from marks caused by sticks and stones, and yet carry festering wounds caused by words that <u>did</u> hurt us. Not long ago in a seminar, I complimented one of the attendees on her appearance. Her response surprised me. With her eyes looking at the floor she said, "I'm ugly." I asked her what she meant, and she told me that in high school her girlfriend had relayed a comment to her that was supposedly from a boy she liked. Her girlfriend said, "John says you have a great body, but you have a horsey face." She didn't. She was attractive, well dressed, and well spoken. Yet, a careless remark made over thirty years ago had set the tone for her self–image. Many of us carry emotional scar tissue caused by childhood chants like, "Fatty, fatty, two–by–four," "Four eyes, four eyes," or those that pick on some other area of our anatomy like our nose, our ears, or the color of our skin.

As we grow up, careless words spoken by fools are no less damaging to our self–esteem or our reputation. A young man I used to know was accused by his boss of stealing his wallet. He stated that the wallet was on his desk and now it was gone, that the only other person having entered the office was that young man, and it was obvious that the young man must have stolen the wallet. The young man was dismissed and the word went out that he was a thief. Two days later, the boss found the wallet where it had fallen down into one of the desk drawers. He was ashamed of his actions, called the young man, and pleaded for his forgiveness. The young man returned to work. The boss called a meeting and explained the mistake he had made to everyone. He even gave the young man a bonus. No harm done. Right? Wrong, for some will not hear the retraction.

A Rabbi found himself in a similar situation. One of his villagers had made untrue statements about him. When the villager found they were untrue, he went to the Rabbi. He promised to stand up before the town and admit that he was wrong, to retract all of his words. The Rabbi said he could repair the damage if he could perform one task. He should take a feather pillow into the town square, open it up, and shake the feathers into the wind. Then he should collect each and every feather and return the pillow, intact, to the Rabbi. The villager said to the Rabbi, "There is no way, once the feathers are in the wind, that I can get them all back." The Rabbi responded, "Such is it with words, once spoken, they may never be recalled."

The next time we're tempted to use cruel words or to pass on a juicy bit of gossip, we might do well to remember that "Sticks and stones may break my bones, but unkind words can devastate me."

Self–reverence, self–knowledge, self–control,
these three alone lead life to sovereign power.
Alfred, Lord Tennyson

TAPPING THE SUBCONSCIOUS MIND

How much of our activity in an average day do you believe that we consciously control? The best medical and psychological research today states that we control consciously only about 15 percent of our daily actions. The remaining 85 percent are controlled by our subconscious, which we can liken to an airplane's auto–pilot. We have developed habit patterns that allow us to breath, talk, walk, and (if we have a driver's licence) drive.

Driving is a great example, since most of us, in the beginning, had to spend a great deal of time paying attention to our speed and direction. With practice, we became more comfortable and we were able to listen to the radio, talk to a friend, and do other tasks as we drove. The conscious mind had relinquished much of the task of driving to the subconscious. How many of us have had the experience on a long trip, of looking around and wondering what had happened to the past few miles. What happened was our conscious mind was thinking about something else while our subconscious drove merrily along.

The subconscious mind is like a recording device. It can learn only that which the conscious mind provides. Therefore, we must be very careful what we teach it. For example, if I desire to lose weight and yet I walk around telling people, "I just can't lose weight." The subconscious hears, "I just can't lose weight," and does everything possible not to make a liar out of me. We, therefore, must be careful what we allow the subconscious to hear.

Since the subconscious learns by repetition of what it hears, we must teach the subconscious new positive lessons, by repeating them over and over. Here are a few things you may want to consciously say to yourself on a regular basis so that your subconscious will hear it:

1. I am a good and worthwhile person. All who meet me today will be better off for having met me.

2. Because I am a good and worthwhile person, good things will happen to me today.

3. I will give love, and look for its return.

4. I am healthy and happy and choose to feel great.

By taking control of 85 percent of our lives through positive programming of our subconscious, we can lead happier, healthier, and more productive lives. Remember, you are UNIQUE, you are GREAT, and you are SPECIAL. Don't hesitate to tell yourself so.

It is a good thing for an uneducated man to read books of quotations. Bartlett's Familiar Quotations is an admirable work, and I studied it intently. The quotations when engraved upon the memory give you good thoughts. They also make you anxious to read the authors and look for more.

Sir Winston Spencer Churchill

THE WISDOM OF THE AGES

One of my favorite pastimes is to read through Bartlett's Quotations and immerse myself in the wisdom of the ages. Most of the people quoted in Bartlett's and in the other books in my library are scholars, rich, or powerful. Many of them use words of four or more syllables to convey the ideas and thoughts upon which mankind has been built. However, a number of years ago, Roger Smith, the chairman of the board of General Motors, told me something about words that has stayed with me. He said, "Bill, big words fool small people. It's the little words like 'home,' 'mother,' and 'country' that move people. Beware of people who use big words." Since that time, I have looked carefully at the words spoken by many people—eloquent, powerful words like "I have a dream" or "I am a Berliner." Small words with great meaning.

One of my favorite philosophers was a man with little education but a great outlook. His name was Satchel Paige. For those who don't know about Satchel Paige, he was a tremendous pitcher for the Kansas City Monarchs, which was an all-black baseball team. He was one of the first black players to make the big leagues. Satchel had what he called his rules for right living. They were as follows:

1. Avoid fried foods which anger the blood.

2. If your stomach disputes you, lie down and pacify it with cooling thoughts.

3. Go very lightly on the vices such as carrying on in society. The social ramble ain't restful.

4. Keep the juices flowing by jangling around gently while you move.

5. Avoid running at all times.

Satchel didn't have a big word in the bunch. But I think to myself how I wish I had read his philosophy earlier in my life. It might have stopped me from tossing and turning at night after a late night snack of French fries. If we all could learn just to sit back and relax when our stomach disputes us, we could put the Rolaids and Tums people out of business. And those social vices can be killers. Ask anyone who has overindulged at a New Year's Eve party.

Finally, number 4 and 5 work together. Satchel knew that a gentle walk beat that current vice called jogging, and science today is saying that a gentle walk is much better for us than a <u>dead run</u>. Big words fool small people, but Satchel wasn't trying to fool anyone, and we can all profit from his advice.

We secure our friends not by accepting favors but by doing them.

Thucydides

BIG "YOU" — LITTLE "i"

Have you ever noticed how some people seem to be very likeable? They have lots of friends, and people are always trying to do things for them. Have you ever wondered why they are blessed with such riches? Maybe it's not a blessing, maybe they've just discovered the "big YOU, little i" principle and have put it into practice.

Psychologists tell us that in any relationship, both parties must get something. It must be a win–win situation. That is, each party must receive a benefit from the relationship. If our goal is to be better liked and not to be lonely, we must offer something to other people that will make them want to be around us. We can offer them the three most precious gifts that we have. They are:

1. "i" APPRECIATE <u>YOU</u>—Every day people do numerous things for us, most of which we take for granted. Mom helps with our homework. Dad gives us a ride to school. Brother does the dishes, and Sister folds the clothes. Nobody thinks to say, "Thank you." At work, our secretary works late to get the job done. The boss puts us in for a raise. We sweat blood to get a project completed, and nobody thinks to say, "Thank you." It's amazing how much friendship a simple "Thank you" can buy.

To be appreciated, we must first appreciate the works of others. Say, "THANK YOU."

2. "i" NEED YOU—As I travel around the country, the happiest people I have met are those who feel a sense of being needed. Not too long ago, I was doing a program for nursing home personnel and I talked with a number of the older folks living at the nursing home. They said that although they were treated well, the thing they lacked was a sense of being needed. If we know that we're needed, it gives us a sense of importance. We all need to feel important, don't we? Say, "I NEED YOU."

3. "i" LOVE YOU—"Do you love me? Do you love me not? You told me once, but I forgot." Words etched in my memory without the poet's name, yet true just the same. How many of us would give anything to have someone say, "I love you"? Sometimes, we'd trade everything to simply hear the words, "I like you." Strangely enough, love is something pretty hard to give away, for love will ultimately be returned. If we're not getting enough love, most likely we're not giving enough love. We must not assume that people know we love them. Say, "I LOVE YOU," and say it often.

We can't force people to like us. But if we meet their need to be appreciated, to be needed, and to be loved, how can they resist us?

Experience is the name everyone gives to their mistakes.

Oscar Fingal O'Flahertie Wills Wilde

HAVE YOU MADE ANY GOOD MISTAKES LATELY?

A friend of mine is fond of saying, "I never make mistakes. I thought I did once, but I was wrong." Obviously, he was kidding, but some people live their entire lives worried about the possibility that they might make a mistake. Without mistakes, you would be reading this column by lantern light.

Thomas Alva Edison, in his quest to develop a filament for the electric light bulb failed over 4,000 times to find an appropriate material. A newspaperman interviewing Mr. Edison asked him how he could make so many mistakes and cope with so much failure. Mr. Edison replied that he was not a failure, but rather the world's greatest expert on what would not work as a light bulb filament. I agree with Mr. Edison's belief, that a mistake is only proof that someone tried to do something. I further believe that any person who never makes mistakes was hired by someone who did.

Many of today's more enlightened corporate leaders are embracing this philosophy and are openly encouraging their staff to be innovative and to take chances. They are also encouraging them to make mistakes known as early as possible, so that corrective (not punitive) action can be taken. America was, is, and will continue to be a nation built on innovation. We are bound to make mistakes as we travel into uncharted territory.

Charles Kettering may have said it best when he said, "Success is never final, and mistakes are rarely fatal." If we are to achieve success, we must be willing to gamble, to reach out, to try the unknown. Each mistake can be a stepping stone to new knowledge and can strengthen us for future endeavors. Of the ten or twelve self–made millionaires that I have met, the one thing I know that they all have in common is that they have been bankrupt at least once. One of these people has made and lost a million–dollar fortune three times. This gentleman told me, "It's not important how many mistakes I make, but rather what I learn from these mistakes." He then told me the following story.

> A young man went to a wise man and asked him how he could become a success. The wise man answered, "Good judgement." Then the young man asked how to get good judgement. The wise man replied, "Experience." Now the young man asked how he could get experience. The wise man smiled and said, "Bad judgement."

How about you? Have you made any good mistakes lately? Have you made any "bad judgements" that you can turn into useful "experience" so that you can make "good judgements"? Remember, we all have the right to be wrong, but we have the responsibility to learn from our mistakes.

If a man insisted always on being serious, and never allowed himself a bit of fun and relaxation, he would go mad or become unstable without knowing it.

Herodotus

GOING! GOING! GONE FISHING!

In today's world of loud alarm clocks, boom boxes, TV sets, stereos, and of course, the infamous telephone, the stress level continues to build. We feel guilty if we are not engaged in some useful pursuit.

Maybe fishing is an activity that will eliminate your guilt and reduce your stress. There's no room for stress or need for guilt when you go fishing. Unlike golf—where you must continue to hit the ball, or tennis where you have to run all over the court—you can be considered gainfully employed, sitting quietly by a stream, staring absentmindedly at a bobber. You see, if you were lying on a park bench and looking at the sky, you would be accused of loafing. But a bobber in the water legitimizes your effort and no one can criticize you.

I'll never forget a sign that I saw in a boat livery up in Mitchell's Bay, Ontario. The sign simply stated: The gods do not subtract from man's allotted time those days which he spends fishing. If this be the case, I personally have three or four extra years coming.

Now, I know that every time we feel stress closing in on us, we cannot pack up and go fishing. But I do take fishing trips in my mind. I use a relaxation technique called visualization. Visualization is nothing more than a 50-cent word meaning daydreaming. I have found that whenever I feel my muscles tensing as a result of stress, I can control it by doing the following: I first try to find a quiet place, I either sit or lie down, close my eyes, breath in deeply on a three count and slowly exhale on a seven count. I then begin to visualize the beauty of the Gulf of Mexico beach where I enjoy fishing. The picture becomes so real to me that I can hear the waves, smell the salt, and feel the warm sand on my feet. I can see in my mind the white gulls soaring overhead and hear their cries. For just a moment, I am actually there, a thousand miles from whatever troubles are plaguing me. This visualization technique has proven effective in controlling stress and relieving its symptoms. Within minutes, I feel better and can handle the situation at hand.

Each of us has a special place. Maybe it's not a fishing hole. Maybe it's a place from our childhood. Maybe it's being with a friend. If shopping is your thing, maybe it's a walk through Bloomingdales. Whatever the place or situation, being able to return to your "special" place during times of stress will allow you to calm yourself and to make yourself better able to handle the task at hand.

Controlling stress in our society has become a full-time job. We all participate in it. Stress-related illnesses kill more Americans than any other single cause. The next time you feel stress closing in, why not hang up a sign that says: Gone Fishing.

'Tain't worthwhile to wear a day all out before it comes.

Sarah Orne Jewett

"WHAT, ME WORRY?"

"What, me worry?" are immortal words uttered by Alfred E. Newman, spokesman and main cartoon character for MADD magazine. It's easy for a cartoon character to utter such words, and, in the sixties when he uttered them, it was a different time. Today's pace has accelerated rapidly. Problems that weren't even considered in 1960 are now on our doorstep. Yet, maybe Alfred E. Newman's philosophy of not worrying is something that we all should consider. Many of the worries that we take upon ourselves rarely come to be.

President Woodrow Wilson made the statement that if you see four troubles coming down the road, close your eyes. When you open them, three of the troubles will have disappeared. You will be totally unprepared for the one that's left. However, you won't have worried about the other three. It might be that Wilson closed his eyes once too often and that's why he failed in his bid for re-election, but his words do have merit.

Think back over the last year. How many of the things that you worried about did not amount to anything significant? How many nights of sleep did you lose worrying about things that did not happen. If you are normal, probably as many as 80 percent of your worries over the last year will fall into that category. Now, think about all of those things that you worried about over which you had no control. This type of worry is even more debilitating because it adds frustration to the stress factor. Yet, even much of this type of worry will also end with the event not happening, and the worry will have been for naught.

Some years ago, my mother gave my son a gift that brought a piece of valuable philosophy into our family. The gift was a gold medallion inscribed with this prayer written by Reinhold Neibuhr.

> GOD, give us grace
> to accept with serenity
> the things that cannot be changed,
> courage to change the things
> which should be changed,
> and the wisdom to distinguish
> the one from the other.

Each time that we're tempted to worry about some impending disaster, either real or imagined, we are reminded of this philosophy which has become known as the Serenity Prayer. It doesn't always stop us from worrying, but it helps us to put our worry in perspective. It enables us to concentrate our energy on those things over which we have control. We hope that it will add as much to your life as it has to ours, and at least some of the time you will honestly be able to say, "What, me worry?"

If there is anything that we wish to change in the child, we should first examine it and see whether it is not something that could better be changed in ourselves.

Carl Gustav Jung

HOME GROWN CARE BEARS

Over the past several years, all of us have read many articles about the crisis we are facing due to the number of teenage suicides. In some areas, it has grown to epidemic proportions. The use of drugs and alcohol in the teenage population has skyrocketed, and the number of runaways reaching the metropolitan areas are seriously taxing the social agencies set up to assist them.

Why do our young people feel the need to escape through drugs, to run away, and ultimately to commit suicide? What is it in our society that causes such pressures that one would consciously choose to take his/her own life?

Recently, as I walked through a hospital nursery and looked at all of the little faces labeled "Baby Jones," "Baby Smith," or "Baby Mouskewitz," I pondered those very questions. It's hard to put a finger on just when they begin to learn from those around them that; they shouldn't think too much of themselves; they shouldn't be too proud of their accomplishments; and every little imperfection in their physical being (whether real or imagined) is cause for embarrassment. Slowly, insidiously, their sense of self–worth is eroded, until they are left feeling unsure about themselves and their future. Must this always be? Can we change the future?

Certainly, we can make a difference. We can impact on the future by the words we use with our children. We must weigh our words carefully as we talk to our young people. We must make every effort to instill in them a sense of worth. Recently, while walking through a store, I heard a little girl say to her mother, "Mommy, you take care of me and that makes you important. Daddy brings home money for our house and takes care of both of us, and that makes him important. What makes me important?" Her mother replied, "Darling, you are Daddy's and my Care Bear. You always have an unlimited amount of love for us. Whenever we're tired and we need a hug, you're there to love us. You are the most important of all of us."

I watched the little girl's face break into a bright smile and it was all that I could do not to walk over and give the mother a hug myself. This is one parent who, with kind words, is helping her daughter to have a strong sense of self-worth. She is raising a child who will feel good enough about herself to better withstand the lure of drugs and alcohol—a child who, because she feels good about herself, will have the capacity to feel good about others.

Yes, we can change the future! By the words that we use in communicating with our children—by taking time to appreciate them. We must praise their successes and give them encouragement when they fall short. We can change the future if we, too, are willing to home grow CARE BEARS.

Work keeps us from three evils, boredom, vice, and need.

Voltaire

OLD DOES NOT EQUAL WORTHLESS

Things and people become worthless simply because they are old? I think not. Things and people become worthless only when they are of no further use. Things have no choice about whether they have any further use; we make that decision for them. People, on the other hand, make that decision for themselves.

In America today, with rapidly changing technology, many older people have lost their jobs. The resulting trauma causes them to equate growing old with becoming worthless. However, it is not their age but their attitude that has reduced their value. They have scratched themselves from the race before it was even finished. It was Justice Holmes who compared life to a horse race. He pointed out that even at the finish line, the work is not completed. The jockey does not pull the horse up short as he crosses the line, but rather canters on down the track. The race is never over and the work is not finished as long as the will and strength to work remains.

The building of a lifetime does not stop at a certain age. Because I reach 60, 65, or 70 years of age does not buy me a special pass that says I no longer have to be productive or that I may quit learning. Nor does it put up a barrier that stops me from learning or being productive. The choice is always mine.

When I attended night school classes at the University of Dayton, there was one lady who was 84, and her dream was to graduate from the School of Business. Her family had told her that it was silly at her age to spend her time studying for a degree that she would never use. But I wish you could have seen the proud look on their faces as they watched her graduate. They would never have equated the word "old" to the word "worthless," as applied to her. The problem then is not growing old, but maintaining worth. We can do that by continued study and by putting ourselves to service.

Recently, in the Hospice organization, I listened to a retired high-level business executive talk about the satisfaction he received from doing such chores as bathing patients and changing bed sheets. He pointed out that his friends and former co-workers could not understand why he would do such menial chores. They put little or no value upon what he was doing. However, he feels a sense of value, and that is most important.

If you are feeling old and worthless today, it's a good bet that you are not feeling useful. Why not pick up the phone and volunteer with the Cancer Society, Hospice, Heart Fund, or some other worthwhile organization. If earning a living is still a necessity, meet the challenge of technology by enrolling in a night school class to enhance your skills. The key to feeling useful is to be involved, and once you get involved, you'll find that you're not nearly as old as you might think.

There is only one success — to be able to spend your life in your own way.

Christopher Morley

A BLUEPRINT FOR SUCCESS

In numerous seminars over the years, I have asked my audience, "How many of you would like to be successful?" With few exceptions, almost every hand is raised. I then ask the participants to write down how they define success. Most stare blankly at the sheet of paper. Some come up with a general statement such as: I wish to be rich, I wish to be happy, or I want to be important. Few have a specific goal in mind. Those few who do will probably achieve success, and they will be able to identify it when they achieve it.

The following ideas, if applied properly, could be your blueprint to success.

1. Set a specific goal. It is important that we know where we are going. For if we do not, there is little hope that we can get there. If we desire a two–story home, then it should be as real in our mind as we can make it. Cut out pictures of homes that would meet your needs and pin them up around your house so they become a constant reminder. If you wish a boat or a car or any such goal, do the same thing.

2. Establish a plan. Once we know where we're going, then we must commit our energies in such a manner as to get us there. We must

determine what education, effort, and time will be necessary to achieve our goal. Put the plan in writing and review it daily.

3. Build a desire. Many people set goals, create a plan, and fail because they do not build a desire. When we first establish a goal, desire is like a small flame. Without effort, it will go out. But if you fan the flame, by looking at the pictures you have around the house, by sharing your goal with others, and by fixating on the good things to come upon achieving your goal, desire will burst into a magnificent blaze.

4. Develop confidence. There will always be people who tell us it can't be done. If our belief in them is greater than our belief in ourselves, we will give up and we will fail. Surround yourself with people who will support you in your quest.

5. Never give up. We must develop a persevering attitude that causes us to take one step and then another, to reach for the impossible, and then to touch it. Keep on trying.

Each of us is the master craftsman of our own life. It is solely up to us what we do with the building materials we are given. And, in the end, we are the only one who will be held accountable.

A lifetime of happiness! No man alive could bear it: it would be hell on earth.
George Bernard Shaw

"BEWARE THE CALM SEA"

The crews of the old sailing vessels had a saying: "Beware the calm sea." It may sound funny that sailors would dread the calm sea. One would think they would dread the storm and the violent ocean that it creates. It was, however, the dead calm that struck fear in the heart of the sailor, because it was the time that the ship sat motionless, a time of monotony and boredom. One only has to read the "Rhyme of the Ancient Mariner" to feel the effect of a calm sea on a sailor.

Some of my friends who sail say that they are most alive when the winds are high, the waves are rough, and they are pitting their skill, and even their lives, against nature. On the other hand, the tedium of a calm sea, day after day, week after week, has literally caused men to go mad.

Many of us in today's society are living in what amounts to a calm sea. We have achieved much. Our jobs are going well. Our homes are paid for. Our children are grown. We do the same job day after day, week after week. We associate with the same people, attend the same church, clubs, and organizations. We have attained the great American dream of being successful.

The other day at lunch, a friend of mine seemed somewhat depressed and I asked him what his problem was. He said, "I don't have any problems, and that's my problem." He said that his company was running smoothly and he had achieved all of his goals. He and his family were going busily about their lives and he was, in fact, just plain bored. He confided in me that he was about to do some things, just for the fun of it, in order to bring some excitement into his life. The plan he outlined was sure to be destructive to both him and his family. He had met the calm sea, and it was winning.

The challenge he faced was the one that we all face when we accomplish our goals and find ourselves on the calm sea of success. That challenge is not to let success ruin us. The absence of problems removes the excitement from our lives. Where there is no risk, there is no excitement. We talked some more and my friend began to see that what he needed to do was to establish new worthy goals, and not to fall into the trap of excitement for excitement's sake. People need problems to solve, mysteries to unravel, and victories to achieve. The Chinese have a curse that says, "May you live in interesting times." I believe the true curse would be, "May you live in uninteresting times." But whatever the time is for you, beware the calm sea.

Life that dares send a challenge to his end, and when it comes, says, "Welcome, friend!"
Richard Crashaw

SPARKLE OR FIZZLE, IT'S YOUR LIFE

There is an old prayer which simply states, "God, don't let me die until I'm dead." A great many people walk around every day in a state of semi-consciousness. They have lost their zest for life and find it difficult, if not impossible, to get excited about anything.

Has your life become a chore rather than a pleasure? Have you noticed that your life is more fizzle than sparkle? Are you slipping into a dull, gray world of boredom and tedium? If so, isn't it time to climb out of the shadows and into a world that can be bright, exciting, and new?

I remember a 70-year-old woman named Mary, who created her own bright and exciting world, and maybe her story will help us begin our climb. She once told me not to be fooled by her wrinkles, that no matter how old she looked, a young girl was still inside. As I got to know her better, she grew younger and younger in my eyes. She combined the best of mature wisdom with youthful exuberance. She rarely talked of yesterday, but always had time to discuss plans for tomorrow. I don't remember a time when she did not have a dream—a goal yet to be achieved. She was a voracious reader, and she could discuss peonies or politics with equal vigor. In fact, she could and would take either side in any discussion. Her days were spent doing the most mundane of tasks, and yet she set a challenge for herself to find new and unique ways to complete them. In her lifetime, she had lost a son in Korea and a husband to cancer, and yet she never dwelled on her losses, but spoke of the gift she had been given in having had them be a part of her life.

Mary taught me the following things about staying alive all of my life:

1. Growing up does not equate to growing old. Adults can swing on swings, ride bikes, and walk barefoot through puddles, for these are not the exclusive domain of the young.

2. Maturity does not exclude enthusiasm. Let words like "Wow!" "Neat!" and "Super!" pop into your vocabulary.

3. Boredom is not in the task, but in the doer. The creative capacity of the mind, when put into use, can turn even the most mundane of tasks into an exciting challenge.

4. Yesterday is gone. Tomorrow is a promise. But today is ours. We have twenty–four gleaming hours each set with sixty shining minutes, to add sparkle to our lives, depending upon how we use them.

Mary lived her entire life, and didn't die until she was dead. I pray that each of us will be so blessed.

The secret of success is constancy of purpose.
Benjamin Disraeli

DO YOU HAVE A PICTURE OF SUCCESS?

In my opinion, and that of many notable psychologists, the most important step in achieving success is to have a graphic picture in your mind of what it is that you wish to do, and what you wish to become. When you do this, you bring into play a force that has been called the Power of Positive Imagery. Basically, this power is the ability to create in your mind a firm picture of what you want to accomplish. As you establish a firm picture in your mind of what you hope to achieve, you can begin to actually picture yourself doing it.

For example, when I first decided that I wanted to be a convention and after–dinner speaker, I had trouble picturing myself walking out in front of a large audience. Let's face it, I got sweaty palms thinking about walking out in front of an audience of friends and neighbors. When someone asked me what I did for a living, I would tell them that I wrote a few programs, did some photography, and "Oh yes! I did speak some." It wasn't until I fully visualized myself as a speaker that our business began to flourish. I began to picture myself as a speaker and to refer to myself as a speaker. I painted a picture in my mind of a large hall, jammed with applauding people. I saw myself walking out on the stage and hearing thunderous applause, and as I spoke, they hung on every word, laughing and crying on cue as

I moved them with my oratory. And I pictured them giving me a standing ovation as I finished. These pictures became so vivid that it was just like facing a real audience; my hands would shake, my pulse rate would rise, and my shirt would be wet with perspiration when I finished. And yet each time that I would run the picture through my mind, the task became easier. I pictured the welcoming applause a little louder each time; I kept adding more and more smiling faces to the group; and because it was my dream, I made the standing ovation even more thunderous.

Then the opportunity came to face the greatest challenge of my career. I was hired to speak before 3,000 people at the Performing Arts Center in Nashville, Tennessee. As I walked out onto that stage, it was my dream come true. I felt like I belonged there, because I had been there so many times in my dream. I was prepared. I was ready. My hands were dry. My pulse rate was down. I had the confidence necessary to live up to their expectations and, more importantly, to my own.

The Power of Positive Imagery is one which can be put to use by any person of any age. The Japanese little league teams have had tremendous success using the Power of Positive Imagery. Before a youngster takes his first swing with a bat, his coach has him go through an exercise in which he visualizes himself hitting the ball. Each of us has the ability to hit the ball any time we choose to do it, but first we must see ourselves doing it. The ball's in your court. Can you see yourself hitting it? If you can, you will.

The difference between the impossible and the
possible lies in a man's determination
Tommy Lasorda

THE BASIC INGREDIENTS

In Norman Vincent Peale's book, <u>Stay Alive All Your Life,</u> he tells the story of a man who went from being a defeated mop pusher to becoming a successful restaurant owner, armed solely with his desire to succeed and his strength of belief in himself. Printed on his menus were these lines that had inspired him, and he hoped they would have the same effect on his customers:

> If you think you are beaten, you are;
> If you think you dare not, you don't;
> If you want to win but think you can't,
> It's almost a cinch you won't.
> If you think you'll lose, you're lost;
> For out in the world we find
> Success begins with a fellow's will;
> It's all in the state of the mind.
> Life's battles don't always go
> To the stronger and faster man,
> But sooner or later the man who wins
> Is the man who thinks he can.

Throughout history, the lesson has been the same. It is not always the fastest, the strongest, or the brightest who wins the race and reaps the reward. Five hundred years before Christ, Aesop told the fable of "The Tortoise and the Hare." Any intelligent person would have bet on the hare to win. He had the speed, endurance, and general racing ability to leave the tortoise way behind. What he didn't have was the commitment to win the race. The tortoise, on the other hand, had little speed and no natural racing ability, but he believed he could win the race, and he was committed to doing it. The results of this race are in, and the tortoise won "hands down." He had the desire to win, the will to win, and he made the commitment to win.

Desire, will, and commitment are the basic ingredients, which, when combined, give us the winning edge. It is easy for us to blame our lack of success on the fact that we're not as pretty as someone else, we don't have another's natural athletic ability, or we don't seem to learn as fast. Yet, in the newspaper everyday, we read stories of people who have succeeded against the odds, such as a paraplegic who traveled around the world in his wheelchair, or a person with less than an eighth grade education who started and managed a multi-million dollar company. These people had the desire to win, the will to win, and the commitment necessary to make it happen. Success can be yours when you utilize these same ingredients. Remember, you are unique, you are great, and you are special. You deserve to succeed.

One man has enthusiasm for 30 minutes, another for 30 days, but it is the man who has it for 30 years who makes a success of his life.
Edward B. Butler

TOO OLD TO SIT STILL

While Judy and I were on our way back from the store, I noticed that a friend's motor home was missing from its normal spot in his driveway. Since it is quite large and rarely goes anywhere, its absence was hard to miss. My first thought was that my friend had taken it on vacation. But no, there he was in the garage cleaning up some fishing gear. "Where's the Titanic?" I asked. He replied that she was living up to her name, one given to her because she was so large and because she could go down so quickly. "She's in the shop. Her brakes are frozen and the wheel bearings are making noise. You know she's just too old to sit still so much," he explained. When we returned home, his words echoed in my mind, "just too old to sit still so much."

His words prompted me to remember a lady I had met while waiting for a bus in New York City. Those of you who have tried to get on a bus in New York City know that it is an activity that could easily qualify as an Olympic athletic event. It is one of the best examples of "survival of the fittest" found anywhere in the world. When our bus arrived, I offered to clear the way and help her to get on. She smiled and declined my help. She told me that she had been riding on these busses without help for many years and would have to continue to do so for many years to come. She said that my help would be appreciated today and that she would enjoy it, but if she continued to accept assistance, what began as an enjoyable experience would become a necessity. She explained that the effort she put into coping with each day gave her the ability to do it again the next.

If you're like me, you find it easy to rationalize sitting in an overstuffed easy chair, rather than pursuing a more strenuous activity. After all, the television does nourish our minds, the walking back and forth to the refrigerator does burn calories, and anyone who's tried to open one, knows that pop–top cans can be killers. Somehow though, these rationalizations began to ring hollow as I thought about the old woman and what both she and my friend had said. I thought of the days I had stayed in bed a little longer than I should have, and how I had awakened up stiff and sore. I began to realize the direct relationship between doing nothing and feeling bad. I found that if I exercised one day, I might hurt the next, but that in short order, I could continue to do the strenuous activity and not hurt at all.

Most importantly, I found that the greatest benefit of physical activity was an increase in mental alertness. A brisk walk or a ride on my bicycle has a tendency to blow away my mental cobwebs. I've learned that just like the Titanic, I'm too old to sit still. How about you?

But hushed be every thought that springs from out the bitterness of things.

William Wordsworth

ELIMINATING THE THREE "C's"

Most of us can sail through life on calm waters if we eliminate the use of the three C's—complaining, criticizing, and condemning.

The first of the three C's is complaining. No one likes to be around someone who is constantly complaining. I remember the story of a young monk who had joined an order that required a vow of silence. However, he was allowed to say two words each year on the anniversary of his joining the order. On the first anniversary, the monastery abbot asked him for his two words. He said, "Skimpy food." On the second anniversary he again was asked to speak and he said, "Cold room." Finally, on his third anniversary he said, "I quit." The abbot looked at him with a smile and said, "I'm not surprised. All you've done since you've been here is complain."

The young man had developed a reputation for complaining and had spent three very unhappy years. He had assumed that if he stated the problem, the abbot would come up with the solution. Instead of complaining, had he said, "More food" and "Another blanket," he may well have developed a reputation as a problem solver and had three great years. The secret is not to complain but rather to offer solutions.

The second of the three C's is criticizing. My father was fond of saying that people who criticize are, for the most part, failures. He called them "hasbeens" and "neverwases." They are the "boo birds" who sit in the stands secondguessing and criticizing the people who are playing the game. They are the same people who want to fire a football coach who loses games, even though the coach achieves the primary goal of the game which is to turn out quality young men. If these same people would channel the energy they used to criticize the coach into helping him, they would add a dimension of purpose to their lives, and they would feel a sense of contribution to the community. Successful people look for the good around them and help others to see it. The secret is not to criticize, but to encourage.

The last of the three C's is condemning. Condemnation's only purpose is to destroy. Those who constantly condemn and tear down others are, sooner or later, consumed by their own unhappiness. Because they have broken the biblical admonition to "judge not," they are surrounded by the rubble made of broken dreams and shattered lives. They find that although they have pulled down much, they have built nothing. Successful people look at any endeavor, not to find fault, but rather to build a future. The secret is not to condemn, but to build.

In the end, it's no secret that if we can eliminate the deadly three C's from our lives and become people who are problem solvers rather than complainers, encouragers rather than criticizers, and builders rather than condemners, we will have happier lives.

The gentle mind, by gentle deeds is known.
Edmund Spencer

THE LAST HUG

It had been a great week in Bermuda, and I was the last speaker of the conference. The reaction of the audience had been excellent and how along with 200 members of the Connecticut Credit Union League, I was safely seated in a Delta 1011 winging my way to Boston. All of a sudden, the plane made a very steep bank to the left. Within about two minutes, the captain's voice came over the intercom saying, "Ladies and gentlemen, there is no reason for immediate concern; however, we have received a radio message saying that we may have a device on board that could be hazardous to our health and we are returning to Bermuda."

Once back on the ground, the wife of one of the attendees came to me with the following story. She had missed my seminar and had returned to the hotel just as people were coming out of the meeting room. She didn't know exactly what was happening, but people were hugging each other. Her husband walked straight through the crowd and gave her a great big hug. Since she and her family rarely displayed affection in public, she admonished her husband for hugging her in front of all those people and suggested to him that it could well have waited until they got back to their room or even until later that afternoon, when they returned to their home in Connecticut. In his defense, he explained that Mr. Hodges had asked each participant to hug at least three people immediately following the program, especially those who were very important to them. She said, at the time, that she didn't care what Mr. Hodges said, their family didn't do such things in public. Her story then jumped forward to the captain's voice coming over the loudspeaker and her realization that none of us might live through the night. She explained that immediately, she turned to her husband and in front of those 200 people, gave him a great big hug and even said out loud, "I love you." It became clear to her that hug she had chided him for in the hotel lobby might have been the last hug she ever received. She got a second chance and if we're smart, we will all learn from it. We should never miss a chance to give a hug.

Over the years, I have made hugging a way of life. At a recent conference, a newcomer noticed that a number of people were giving me hugs. He asked one of the other attendees, "Who is that man, and why is everyone giving him a hug?" Her reply was, "He's Bill Hodges and they're hugging him because they know he'll hug them back." I didn't realize quite how much a part of my life it was until one of our friends who has a young son told me that, although her son could not remember my name, he asked, "Could the man who hugs come back?"

In my lifetime, I've been called a lot of things, some good and some bad, but I'm really proud to be known as the man who hugs. However, wouldn't it be great if we all hugged so often that no one would notice a man who hugs? Remember, only the truly strong can afford to be gentle.

Each Person is born to one possession which outvalues all his others — his last breath.
Mark Twain

A DAY WELL SPENT

Have you ever given any thought as to how to judge the value of a day in your life? Do you measure it in the silver and gold that you amass? Do you measure it in the accolades that you receive from others? Or are there other values that make a day a success?

For myself, I judge the value of a day in my life by a series of tests set up by an anonymous poet. The poem is entitled:

A DAY WORTHWHILE

I count that day as wisely spent
In which I do some good
For someone who is far away
Or shares my neighborhood.
A day devoted to the deed
That lends a helping hand
And demonstrates a willingness
To care and understand.
I long to be of usefulness
In little ways and large
Without a selfish motive
And without the slightest charge.
Because in my philosophy
There never is a doubt
That all of us here on earth
Must help each other out.

I feel the day is fruitful
And the time is worth the while
When I promote the happiness
Of one enduring smile.

It would be nice if every day was a day that each of us could devote to helping others, without any thought of promoting ourselves. It is, however, unrealistic. In order for us to be able to spend time helping others, we must first do those things necessary for our own survival. If we are not physically and monetarily healthy, we will not have the strength and resources to be of service to anyone.

Fortunately, earning a living and treating people decently are not mutually exclusive. Each of us has the opportunity every day, with our family, our friends, and our customers, to show that we care. We can, through a variety of actions, show them that we stand with them, that we can be counted upon in times of need. It has been said that we pass this way but once, I believe our challenge is to make each day a day well spent.

Where we love is home — home that our feet may leave, but not our hearts.
Oliver Wendell Holmes

THE GATHERING PLACE

Have you ever wondered what turns a house into a home? What turns one structure on the street into a place where people feel comfortable and wish to gather? I remember as a teenager, that there was one house, one home, at which we kids always gathered. We were drawn there. I don't know exactly why. I don't know if it was the house itself or the family contained within. Maybe it was the spirit of the people, their innate warmth and friendliness.

In this particular home, there was always room for one more. Rarely did a day go by that there was not one extra mouth at the dinner table, and more often than not, several extra mouths. Any of us who have tried to feed teenage boys know that it is not done without some expense and effort. Yet, they never made us feel like we were intruders. The adults in this home seemed to enjoy, and even reveled in, the sounds of youthful exuberance. I can't remember a time that they complained of the radio being played too loud or the noise we created as we indulged in our many activities, most of which were just plain horseplay. These were people with whom we could discuss the problems we faced as we grew up.

Don't get me wrong, my folks were great, but sometimes you just need to talk with someone else—someone who can stand back and look at your problems objectively. Somehow these people made each of us feel special. They made us feel important and truly a part of their family.

In my lifetime, I have had the privilege to meet a number of people like those described above. For the most part, their homes were not the type you might find displayed in magazines like "Better Homes & Gardens." They put emphasis on people rather than on things. The surroundings were comfortable, liveable, and inviting. To them, a manicured yard was not a priority. They knew the dead grass under the tent would grow back and that there would be plenty of time to grow award–winning roses after they had grown a generation of award–winning kids. I remember that they always bought whatever we were selling, for whatever worthy activity we might be representing. In fact, more often than not, they were the ones who volunteered to keep the inventory of candy bars or cookies in their front hall. Even after their kids had graduated, you would see these people sitting in the stands, cheering on school athletic teams.

In the final analysis, I believe that what changes a house into a gathering place is a combination of all of these things. Mostly, it is the people—people who, by their actions, express an open invitation, one that most of us cannot resist. However they are able to establish this caring atmosphere, I thank God that they are here.

The man to whom much is given, of him much is required: the man to whom more is given, of him much more is required.

THE POWER TO CHOOSE

While walking through the beautiful park behind my home, I noticed several large, buzzard–like birds circling in the distance. These birds circled lower and lower until they finally landed and began picking at something on the ground. As I walked closer, I startled them and they flew away. What they had been eating was the partially decomposed carcass of a very dead rabbit. As I walked further along the path, I also chanced to see a very rare sight. It was a hummingbird, flapping its tiny wings so fast that one could scarcely see them. It was savoring the nectar of a small wild flower.

It struck me funny that these two birds—one with mighty wings that could have taken it anywhere—had chosen to eat a partially rotted meal, and the other—with tiny wings—had used them to find a meal consisting of the nectar of the gods. As I continued my walk, I thought about how these birds, each in its own way, was a lot like some of the people that I knew. Some of the strongest and most able of my acquaintances have done little with what they had been given. And yet, once in a while, I meet a man who has been given very little, at least in physical ability, and this man shows me how much a human being can accomplish. Such a man is Jerry Traylor.

Jerry was born with cerebral palsy, and as a result, has almost no use of his legs. As a child, he underwent more than 14 corrective surgeries, and he spent most of his youth in body casts, body braces, or leg braces. As an adult, Jerry still walks with the assistance of crutches. Most of us would not picture a man with these physical limitations when the words "cross–country runner" are mentioned. Yet, Jerry Traylor has done what most of us who are able bodied would not consider doing. Jerry began and completed what he called his "trail of new beginnings." Jerry began his trail by competing in over 22 marathons. He has met the challenge of Pike's Peak, not once but three times. And yet, there are people who, because he moves on crutches, automatically set limits for him. Jerry is a no–limit person. He displayed that when he began running in San Francisco and ended up, 3,000 miles later, in New York City. Dr. Norman Vincent Peale said of Jerry, "He is a motivational doer. He is most convincing when he tells people what it takes to achieve difficult goals, for they know he has achieved many." Jerry Traylor's legs can be compared to the wings of the hummingbird. He has done much with fragile legs. He has conditioned them to go far beyond what could be reasonably expected.

When I first saw Jerry, I have to admit that I pitied him. But within minutes of meeting him, my pity turned to envy. He is a bright, shining example of what any of us can be, if we simply make the most of what we are given.

Big doors swing on little hinges.

W. Clement Stone

JUST A ...

While standing in a business establishment, I was having a lively discussion with one of the owners. We were enjoying ourselves, and it wasn't until someone else entered the store that I realized that I was blocking the counter. I turned to the new arrival and motioned for her to step in front of me so that she could be served. She smiled at me, pointed at the proprietor and said, "She's just a friend." I questioned the words, "just a friend." The visitor did not see the point I was making and responded with, "She's just a good friend." I asked her how many good friends she had, that she could refer to this friend as "just" a good friend? Although the friendship was very important to her, she used a word to describe it which is commonly thought of as a putdown.

Many of us do the same thing every day. We refer to ourselves as "just" a mechanic, "just" a secretary, "just" a housewife, "just" a teacher, or "just a ..." Every time we do this to ourselves, we put ourselves down a little bit. Our mind hears that we're not very important. It hears that we don't think very much of ourselves. We lose a little bit of the pride that we should have in who we are and what we are.

There are those who will read this and think to themselves, "How can such a small, insignificant phrase have any impact upon our self esteem?" In answer to those people, I would like to quote from

W. Clement Stone's great book, <u>The Success System That Never Fails.</u> In this book, Mr. Stone makes the point that, "Big doors swing on little hinges." It is not always the big things in life that cause us the greatest difficulties. Many times, it's the small things. How many of you have elephant repellent in your medicine chest? Not too many, I'll bet. On the other hand, I would be willing to wager that many of you have insect repellent on hand. You can see an elephant coming, and get out of his way. It's the little insects that cause us the most trouble. So it is with the power of words. One small word, repeated over and over, can impact profoundly upon our life.

The next time that you are tempted to modify a reference to yourself, or to someone you care about, with words such as "only," "merely," or the insidious "just," think about the seeds that you are planting. What type of fruit will these seeds bear? Will your words make yourself or others feel better or worse? I know of no friend, customer, or relative who would not appreciate being referred to as a good friend, a good customer, or a good wife, daughter, or son. Words are important, and the words we use paint a graphic picture of how we feel about ourselves and those around us. By eliminating negative words from our speech, that picture will shine brightly for all to see.

There is a tide in the affairs of men which,
taken at the flood, leads on to fortune; omitted,
all the voyage of their life is bound in shallows
and in miseries.

William Shakespeare

THE TIDES OF LIFE

In his play "Julius Caesar," Shakespeare wrote, "There is a tide in the affairs of men which, taken at the flood, leads on to fortune; omitted, all the voyage of their life is bound in shallows and in miseries." Taken literally, it appears that Shakespeare believed opportunity knocks but once, and if we miss our chance, it will never knock again. I have had the opportunity to know many people who have, by their actions, shown they agreed with Shakespeare. They spent a considerable amount of time telling everyone about the great opportunity they once had, and how if they had only taken it, they would now be rich or famous. In fact, they spend so much time dwelling on their missed opportunity of the past, that they fail to see the opportunities which are presented to them in the here and now.

It is my feeling that Shakespeare was correct in comparing opportunity to the tide. However, his analogy breaks down when we remember that the tide comes in and out, not once but normally several times every day. Opportunity is exactly like the tide. Just as the tide comes in and out every day, so does opportunity. Those who know the tides realize that there are high and powerful tides and there are also low tides. So it is with opportunity. Each day we are faced with challenges. Each of these challenges, whether great or small, provides an opportunity for us to learn, grow, and prosper. In my own life, I have had many opportunities, some that I saw and some that slipped right past me. Whoever it was who said, "Opportunity knocks but once," just wasn't listening. For most of us, opportunity not only knocks, but literally tries to kick the door down. Unfortunately, many of us, for a variety of reasons, are afraid to answer the door.

Opportunity rarely comes to our door dressed as prosperity. More often, it comes disguised as hard work. It generally requires some risk of our time, capital, and/or personal comfort. Those who would sit on the pier waiting for their ship to come in may find themselves missing the boat. Truly successful people swim out to meet the boat. They're not afraid to get wet in pursuit of their goals. They're not afraid to get involved in life, to expend effort, or to take risks.

In 1870, more than 200 years after Shakespeare, James Russell Lowell wrote these words in one of his essays: "Truly, there is a tide in the affairs of men, but there is no gulf stream setting forever in one direction." Opportunities missed yesterday will be replaced by those presented today. Our responsibility is not to dwell upon missed opportunities but rather to listen carefully for the "knocking" of new ones. Fate will never condemn us to the shallows and miseries of misfortune, but rather, how we react to fate will choose our destination.

*An idea whose time has come will find a way
to achieve it.*

W. N. Hodges

THE IDEA OF THE WEEK

One of the top speakers in America today is a gentleman by the name of Ira Hayes. Ira has been sharing success ideas with audiences for over 30 years. In fact, it was Ira who at a success rally in the early 70's prompted me to take the career path that I have taken. In the more than 10 years that have followed, he has given me much sound advice and today I would like to share some of it with you.

Ira is a very enthusiastic person. In fact, he has been given the title "Ambassador of Enthusiasm" by his friends. He believes in the power of being positive and he pointed out to me that a negative person is very much like the defense on a football team. Their primary goal is to stop someone from doing something. The defense rarely scores, and neither does a negative person. When the defense does score, it's always by accident and not the result of a scoring plan. So it is true with negative people. In the game of football, a defensive team is useful and necessary. But in the game of life, most negative people simply get in the way of those who are building the future.

The greatest idea that Ira has given to me is his "Idea Book." How many times have you had a great idea, one that you just knew was going to make you a success, one that you were going to begin working on just as soon as you got the time, one that right now you can't quite seem to remember? If you are normal, you have had ideas like that and have lost them forever because you didn't write them down. Ira suggests that we keep a spiral binder and number the lines in it from 1 to 52. We then sit down every week and write down our idea of the week. Sometimes you may have a really big idea, so you may want to leave two lines, or even three if you think very big. Over a years time, you will have collected 52 good ideas. In 10 years, you will have 520 good ideas. Certainly, one of those has the potential to make you rich and famous.

Ira, when asked one day how he planned to accomplish an idea he had written down, smiled at the questioner and responded, "I told you this was an 'Idea Book,' not a 'How You're Going to Do It Book.'" You see, it's not important that you be able to do the idea today, but rather that you write it down today. An idea that you may not have the resources for today may well become possible next year, but it cannot be done if you don't remember the idea.

Some years ago, I started my own "Idea Book." At the time I was in an audience listening to Ira present his program, "Keeping Pace with Tomorrow." I started the book with a single entry. That entry was "Create an idea book." Tonight when you lay this column down, why not find a piece of paper and start your own book with the same idea?

Genius is nothing but a greater aptitude for patience.

Georges De Buffon

DON'T PUSH

While officiating a football game, one of the other officials pointed out to me that a dog had come on the field. Because of the hazard to the players and to the animal, we had to stop play and remove the dog from the field. Stopping play was easy. Removing the dog was not. My friend decided that he would chase the dog from the field. The dog decided my friend was playing with him, and stayed just out of his reach. The harder my friend tried to catch the dog, the more determined the dog was not to be caught.

You can imagine the kind of advice and encouragement this man in a black and white shirt was receiving from the stands. From the comments, I believe everyone was on the side of the dog.

Finally, one young cheerleader asked if she could try to catch the animal. We agreed and she asked us to stand back as she walked out into the center of the field and sat down. She made no attempt to chase the animal. In fact, she hardly acknowledged its existence. The animal, on the other hand, looked at her in a rather puzzled manner. What was this human being doing, sitting in the middle of the field? Within three minutes, the dog's natural curiosity caused him to walk up to the girl who was ignoring him. He still wanted to play and began nuzzling her. She deftly reached out, collared the dog, and led him from the field.

When the game was over, I had an opportunity to talk with the young lady. I asked her where she had gotten the idea to capture the dog in that manner. She replied that playing in her grandmother's garden, she had chased all over after butterflies, and had learned that no matter how hard she pushed, they would always stay just out of her grasp. One day, having worn herself out from running after the butterflies, she had sat down exhausted, fully intending to take up the chase after she had rested. While sitting there quietly, one of the butterflies gently fluttered over to her and landed on her hand. She said that she learned then that some things could not be accomplished by force but rather must be accomplished by patience.

Many of us have not learned this lesson. We are like the rat that runs in the circular cage—much noise and fury—running hard but getting nowhere. Success eludes us and stays just out of our grasp. The harder we push, the more it seems to shy away from us. Maybe we all should take a lesson from the young woman and her butterfly. When we've put out as much effort as possible, done everything we know how to do, maybe it's time to sit down and wait. Maybe it's time to listen to others when they tell us, "Don't push."

No man is worth his salt who is not ready at all times to risk his body, to risk his well being, to risk his life, in a great cause.

Theodore Roosevelt

TRAVEL AT YOUR OWN RISK

Recently, while riding through a rural Ohio county, I noticed the roads were a bit rough and occasionally at the side of the road was a sign proclaiming, "TRAVEL AT YOUR OWN RISK." I'd seen that sign before and dismissed it from my mind. But later in the day, I was joking with a client about his backwoods community that couldn't even provide a decent road. He explained that the people had rejected additional requests from government for more money and had decided to put up with rougher roads in return for less government interference in their lives.

Riding home that day, I saw that sign again and, for some reason, my mind drifted back in history to the docks of England where people were leaving for a new land. Surely as they boarded the ships, there must have been a sign proclaiming, "TRAVEL AT YOUR OWN RISK." I thought too of those folks, not unlike you or me, who loaded all of their worldly belongings into wagons and headed west into a strange and hostile land armed only with their dreams. Surely, as they pulled out of St. Louis, the last thing they saw was a sign proclaiming, "TRAVEL AT YOUR OWN RISK."

Today in America, the sign goes back up. The spirit that gave courage to those early pioneers is being reactivated across our country. In cities like ours we, as individual citizens, must take the lead in providing collective and individual services to our friends and neighbors.

We can do this by taking an active interest in the happenings of our government and by sharing our time and talents with philanthropic and charitable organizations. We can reawaken in America the same spirit that caused neighbor to help neighbor when it came to harvesting crops or raising a barn. John Kennedy said, "Ask not what your country can do for you, but rather what you can do for your country." In today's world, I believe the statement should read, "Ask not what your country can do for you, but rather what you can do for yourself." If we begin doing for ourselves, government will not be tempted to step in and fill the void.

What I first saw as a sign of failure in that small rural community, I have come to believe was a declaration of faith in their own ability to survive without big brother. As each of us go down life's road, we shouldn't damn the potholes; they let us know we're making progress. Let us thank God every day that we still live in a country where the sign reads, "TRAVEL AT YOUR OWN RISK."

This is the day which the Lord hath made; we will rejoice and be glad in it.

Psalms 118:24

WOULD YOU BE THE ONE?

A friend of mine told me a story about a New York broker who had lost everything when the stock market plunged 500 points in October of 1987. According to my friend, the broker had invested heavily in the market and when it plunged, he lost all that he had accumulated over a number of years. He was very despondent and in his grief, decided to end his life. He looked out his office window which was 35 floors above the street, and pondered the thought of jumping. His mind said, "Jump!" But deep down, another voice within him said, "Those are innocent people down below. If you jump, you might harm one of them."

To satisfy this inner conflict, he decided not to jump but rather to walk down to the East River and throw himself in. As he walked along, he began to rethink his decision. Were things as bad as he thought? Was he alone? Did nobody care? He began to wonder if he wasn't overreacting. He decided that as he walked toward the East River, if just one person would smile, wave, or in some friendly manner, recognize his existence, that he would not end his life.

WOULD YOU HAVE BEEN THE ONE?

Would you have been the one to take time out of your busy schedule, out of today's hustle and bustle, to smile at a stranger? Would you have been the one to sense his despondency? Would you have been the one to reach out to help another human being? I think that each of us would like to believe that we are the kind of person who would help someone we see is in need.

The problem today is that in our highly mobile, isolated, fast–paced, and overcrowded society, we become so tied up in the competition that we don't see those who are falling behind. We walk through crowds of people, avoiding any kind of eye contact, pretending that if we don't see them, they're not there. And yet, as I travel the sidewalks of America, I have found a unique truth. The truth is if I smile and say "Hello" to a stranger, the stranger will smile and return the greeting.

It's amazing how good it makes you feel to know that your simple "Hello" and smile has changed a glum face into a bright and shining one. Oh, I'm not telling you that you won't surprise somebody, and you may even get some puzzled looks, but the rewards are worth the effort. I have never yet had anyone reply negatively when I have given them a hearty "Good Morning." Over a period of time, some who were simply "good morning acquaintances" have become "personal friends."

I believe that you can add much to your life by bringing sunshine to the lives of others. Remember, you can be the one who makes a difference. SMILE!!

I have lost friends some by death — others by my sheer inability to cross the street.
Virginia Woolf

DEFEATING LONELINESS (Part I)

For most of us, the holiday season is a time of joy, happiness, and good cheer. We surround ourselves with our friends and family and forget that many in this country are suffering from one of the great debilitating diseases—loneliness. For them, any holiday season is just another time period when they are on the outside looking in. It is to these people that I would like to give the following ideas about how to break the loneliness cycle.

1. Like yourself. Since all of us spend more time alone than we do with other people, it is imperative that we develop a deep and abiding sense of self–respect. To do this, we must give ourselves good and positive counsel. We must tell ourselves good things, not bad things. Consider, would you hang around someone who is constantly calling you stupid, dumb, or ugly? I think not. If you're saying these things about yourself to yourself, it is not hard to understand why you don't enjoy your own company. Remember, speak positively in all of your self–talk. When you do this, you will become your own best friend and a great companion.

2. Maintain contact. Maintaining contact with friends who have moved away is a powerful tool for giving ourselves a sense of continuity. You say

you write letters, but people don't write back, and you can't understand why. More often than not, we should seek the answer to this question in the letters that we have written. We have a friend, who over the years, has written us numerous letters, and although we love the friend, we do not look forward to receiving his letters. During the 20 years we have received his letters, we cannot remember reading about any of the good things that have happened in his life. When things aren't going badly for him, he usually chooses some dark item from the news to talk about. As a result of these negative letters, we do very little to encourage him to write again. On the other hand, we have another friend who takes an active interest in our life, and in each of her letters, asks many questions about what we're doing. She shares her joys, large and small, and we look forward to receiving letters from her. Since we believe in the old adage, "You have to give to get," we respond to her letters almost immediately. I don't know how many other people she corresponds with, but I doubt that she ever has to face an empty mailbox. She has learned that good news is always welcome. These are but two ideas to help defeat one of the most debilitating maladies known to man—loneliness. On the next page, we will look at other suggestions that may help brighten the lives of those willing to make the investment in their own well-being.

The only way to have a friend is to be one.
Ralph Waldo Emerson

DEFEATING LONELINESS (Part II)

On the previus page, we talked about finding solutions for loneliness. The first solution was to develop a healthy sense of self–respect so that you could be your own best friend. The second was to nurture "positive" correspondence with friends and family who have moved away. In addition, these ideas may prove helpful:

1. Expand your circle of friends. Where does one go to find a friend? The best place to go is to a group, club, or organization that shares your interests, background, and moral standards. No matter what your interest, someone has probably formed a group of which you can be a part. To find this group, you can begin by looking in the Yellow Pages of your telephone book. For example, the phone book in my desk drawer has a full page of associations and over ten pages of churches. The library has a directory of over 7,000 national associations. Somewhere in there, there has to be a subject in which you are interested. Another option is to call your Chamber of Commerce and ask them for a list of the local groups that meet in your area. If you are too shy to go alone, call one of the officers of the group, or the pastor if it's a church, and find out what provision they have for assigning a sponsor to potential members. Many times,

someone will come and pick you up at your home, take you to the meeting, introduce you around, and then take you home. Remember, the best way to have a friend is to be one, and you can't do that sitting home alone.

2.   Share your talents. The happiest and most productive people that I know are those who have learned to use whatever talent they have for the good of those around them. One of our neighbors, who has been retired for some time, is never lonely. There is always someone knocking on his door for advice. He always seems to have time to answer questions, to take something apart, or to put it back together. He never makes it seem as though we're burdening him, or that we are stupid because we don't know how to fix something. By sharing his talents, he has become a very important part of our lives and our neighborhood. Many older people complain that no one comes to see them. Yet, in our neighborhood, on any nice evening, you will see this man and his wife on their front porch surrounded by neighbors. Remember that somewhere, someone needs your talents. Are you ready to give?

As we begin to feel good about ourselves, we will lose the fear we might have of presenting ourselves to others; then by maintaining positive correspondence, joining groups, and sharing our talents, we will expand our relationships and give purpose to our lives. Those with a sense of purpose rarely have time to be lonely.

No act of kindness, no matter how small, is ever wasted.

Aesop

A CHRISTMAS STORY

The holiday season causes people to do many things that they might not otherwise do—most of them good. We see people who sacrifice their own desires to be able to buy presents for others. We also see people banding together for no other purpose than to celebrate the season. My story falls somewhere in between.

On a cold winter night many years ago, I was attending a Christmas party. Much of the spirit that was in the room was not "Father Christmas," but "Old Grand Dad." It was not so much a Christmas party as it was a reason to get together, until someone suggested we go caroling. For some reason, the very suggestion of going caroling put the whole purpose of the party into perspective. Our host handed each of us a flashlight and a song sheet. Fortified from the wassail bowl, we trudged out into the snow.

The reactions we received from the people we serenaded were varied. Some turned out their porchlights and pretended they weren't home. One came out with a few coins wanting to donate to whatever cause we represented (I think he was hoping he could buy us off). Others simply stood in the doorway and shook their heads. At the time, I thought they were in awe of our singing, now I'm not sure that awe is the appropriate word.

As the evening wore on, the spirits we were fortified with began to wear off, and our host was faced with a possible mutiny amongst his carolers. In fact, we had decided to quit when he pleaded with us to try just one more song at one more house. The only song we had not sung was one which was written in German on our songsheets. It was entitled "Oh! Tannenbaum." We decided that even though none of us spoke German, if we were going to sing one more song, that would be it.

We rang the doorbell, and a white haired gentleman answered the door. As one, we began to sing and almost immediately tears began to roll down his cheeks. By this time, I had a suspicion that our singing wasn't great, but I really didn't think it was so bad as to cause pain. When we finished the song, he asked us to wait. In a few minutes, he returned with his wife and asked us to sing the song again. After we completed our song, he explained that he was a liaison officer in the German Air Force. He and his wife had just arrived in our country, and since they had not yet made any friends, they were very homesick. He said that our gift of song had made them feel the spirit of Christmas and not so much alone.

It's ironic that what started out as a lark turned out to be a gift. We made Christmas a reality for them, and their reaction to what we did made Christmas real for us.

TO-MORROW you'll reform you cry; in what far country does this morrow lie.

Poor Richard's Almanac

THIS YEAR, I PROMISE TO .....

On January 1 every year, I make statements to myself like:

1. "This year, I promise to exercise on a regular basis."

2. "This year, I promise to eat more fruits and vegetables and fewer pies and cookies."

3. "This year, I am going to lose the 20 extra pounds I carry."

4. "This year, I'm going to slow down and enjoy life."

5. "This year, I'm going to save money for my old age."

6. "This year, I'm going to quit putting things off."

The last of these will be the first resolution broken. You see, over a period of years, I have learned to know myself very well. I know for a fact that I will delay implementing each of these promises and that the end of the year will find me with most of them unfulfilled.

Why make resolutions if I am not going to keep them? The answer to that is found in human nature. If a person has no goals, he or she is certain to achieve them. On the other hand, if one has some goal, there is a better than even chance that at least part of it will be accomplished. If I promise to spend three hours every other day at the gym, I will most probably find a thousand reasons why the commitment cannot be kept. But the guilt felt because that commitment is not kept may at least cause me to take a walk.

Regarding resolution #2, if I could keep it, I would not have nearly as much trouble with resolution #3. But every time I am reminded of it, it becomes more difficult for me to choose an apple over a "Twinkie." In the past years, Twinkies have won two to one, but it could have been three to none.

As far as slowing down and enjoying life, I've got a handle on that. However, #5 gets in my way and causes the nagging feeling that I shouldn't enjoy too much at the expense of security. Oh well, back to work. Resolutions for the New Year are great as long as they're kept in the proper perspective. They should be reasonably achievable, sanely implemented, and logically suited to our goals. We should keep in mind that the value of a resolution is not in whether it was totally fulfilled, but rather whether it moved us in the right direction. If it made us healthier, happier, and more productive, then it was a great "I promise to ...."

A "Man" can be destroyed but not defeated.
Ernest Hemingway

THE SEED

Have you ever had the opportunity to visit the Redwood Forest on our California coast? If you have, it's a sight that you will not forget, and if you haven't, it's a trip that you owe to yourself. Those trees are the largest living objects on the face of the earth.

One of them is affectionately called "The General Sherman." It is almost 300 feet high. That's as tall as a football field is long. It measures over 36 feet across and would require more than 20 people to hold hands around it. If it were cut down and made into lumber, it would take more than 200 railroad cars to haul the lumber away. The General Sherman is over 3,000 years old. As I stood looking at this tree, all of these facts crossed my mind, but the most impressive fact of all was that this tree started life as a seed weighing less than 1/1000 of an ounce. That's so small that thousands of them would fit in the palm of your hand. Yet, from this small beginning sprang this giant. It is a perfect example of the fact that it's not where you begin, but rather where you end up that counts.

Each of us has much in common with the General Sherman. We begin as small seeds and grow into adult human beings. We are subjected to a diversity of environments and a variety of conditions that can either facilitate or retard growth. Were the General Sherman to be cut down, we would be able to see, by examining its growth rings, how it had been affected by environmental conditions over its 3,000–year lifetime. In years with conditions good for growth, the growth rings would be far apart, and in the years of drought, the tree would go dormant for self–protection and the rings would be much closer together. But in either case, there would still be growth.

It is more difficult to determine how human beings have been affected by their environment. We do know human beings, not unlike the General Sherman, go dormant when conditions are not favorable for growth. There are times in our lives when we just can't put things together; we're in the wrong job, have marital problems, are overextended and underfunded. We feel like we are shoveling sand against the tide and the tide is winning.

It is at this time, when it is most important to plan our moves and our lives from an intellectual rather than an emotional standpoint. We may have to give a little, rather than standing firm. The General Sherman, in a high wind, will sway more than 20 feet from centerline. If it did not sway, it would break.

So it is with most of us. It is also true with us that even though we may have to bend in adversity, we—like the General Sherman—will, sooner or later, stand tall again. These are the times that we must take the problems of life in stride and conserve energy until the next growing season. Remember, even in adversity, there will be growth.

SUCCESS comes before WORK only in the dictionary.

Anon

WHY PEOPLE SUCCEED

"Luck"—we give it credit for other's success and blame it for our own failures. There is an old adage that reads, "The harder I work, the luckier I get." The true secret to success is our own effort, not the four-leaf clover, rabbit's foot, or charm we carry.

Successful people have many things in common. A few of them are listed below. The more of these traits we possess, the more successful we will ultimately become:

1. Do every job as well as it can be done. There is no job too small not to be done right.

2. Find something nice to say about everyone we meet.

3. DO IT NOW. The great thief we all face is one called procrastination. Remember you can't kill time; it's time that kills.

4. Concentrate on improving your strong points. Eighty percent of our success will come from twenty percent of our activity. Concentrate on improving that twenty percent.

5. Be kind to yourself; develop a quiet self-respect.

6. Loyalty is the hallmark of successful people. Build a team of friends upon which to build a life, and then defend them with all of our might.

7. Help others to see their true worth by complimenting them at every opportunity on their strong points.

8. Remain open to suggestion and encourage others to give us their ideas by treating their offerings with respect.

9. When speaking of others, say only those things that you would feel comfortable saying to their face. Remember, a single word spoken carelessly can be more deadly than the sharpest knife to another's self–respect.

10. Finally—There is no "FREE LUNCH." What we get, we will work for. Be willing to give an honest day's work for a day's pay. Be willing to go the extra yard by going to school, going to work early, staying late and, finally, doing those jobs nobody else wants to do.

Few, if any, human beings have been able to totally master this list, and yet those who have tried to live up to its precepts have found that they have led happier, more productive, and more fulfilling lives.

I don't belong to any organized political party.
I'm a democrat.

Will Rogers

CHOOSING A POLITICAL PARTY?

In America, one of the most positive things that we can do is to take part in our nation's political system. To do this, most people join one of the two major political parties. Yet, when I asked people to tell me how I could tell a republican from a democrat, no one explained it quite as well as this description I found in "The Congressional Record."

Democrats buy most of the books that have been banned somewhere.

Republicans form censorship committees and read them as a group.

Republicans are likely to have fewer but larger debts that cause them no concern.

Democrats owe a lot of small bills. They don't worry either.

Democrats give their old clothes to the poor. Republicans wear theirs.

Republicans employ exterminators. Democrats step on bugs.

Democrats name their children after currently popular sports figures, politicians, and entertainers. Republican children are named after their parents or grandparents, according to where the most money is.

Republicans tend to keep their shades drawn,

although there is seldom any reason they should. Democrats ought to, but don't.

Republicans read the financial pages of the newspaper. Democrats put them in the bottom of the bird cage.

On Saturday, republicans head for the hunting lodge or the yacht club, while democrats wash the car and get a haircut.

Republicans raise dahlias, Dalmatians, and eyebrows. Democrats raise beagles, kids, and taxes.

Democrats eat the fish they catch. Republicans hang them on the wall.

Republicans have guest rooms. Democrats have spare rooms filled with old baby furniture.

Democrats suffer from chapped hands and headaches. Republicans have dermatitis and migraines.

Democrats make up plans and then do something else. Republicans follow the plans their grandfathers made.

Republicans sleep in twin beds—some even in separate rooms.

That is why there are more democrats.

After having read this, I'm sure you now know whether you are a republican or a democrat. You may even have opted to become an independent. You see, it really doesn't matter what we call ourselves. What does matter is that good people like you stay involved in the political process.

Never esteem anything as of advantage to thee that shall make thee break thy word or lose thy self–respect.

Marcus Antoninus

THE VALUE OF YOUR WORD

In talking with a sales group, I was trying to impress upon them that the most important asset they had was the value of their word. As I spoke to them, I was reminded of the following story.

Once upon a time, a very wealthy old man was tired of hearing people say he couldn't take it with him, and he devised a plan to do just that. He called together his three most trusted advisors; his pastor, his doctor, and his lawyer. He explained to each of them his plan for taking some of his money with him. The man gave each of his advisors $100,000 in cash with the instructions that at the time of his burial they were each to put $100,000 in his casket just prior to its interment. When the man died and the funeral was held, each of the three gentlemen put a bundle in the casket as promised. As the three of them rode back from the cemetery, the pastor began to cry and confessed to the other two that there had been such need in his parish that he had used half of the money to feed the poor, and he had only thrown in the other half. The doctor then confessed that he had also seen a need and used two–thirds of his money to relieve the suffering of many of the indigent ill in the community. The lawyer sat quietly listening as each of the other two confessed. Finally, he shook his head and said, "I don't know how you two could break the sacred trust and faith of our departed friend and client. For the record, I want both of you to know that I put in a CHECK for the entire amount."

Did the lawyer keep his word? Maybe the letter of the law was served, but the intent of the promise was sorely missed. There are some people in all professions and walks of life who consider themselves honorable because they live up to the letter of their word. Unfortunately, they rarely take into consideration the spirit of the agreement. Because of this, they find that people become wary of doing business with them and their word becomes suspect.

Shakespeare said it best when he said, "And be these juggling fiends no more believ'd, that palter with us in a double sense, that keep the word of promise to our ear, and break it to our hope."

When we give our word to someone, it is imperative that we take into consideration both the letter and the intent of the promise. It is easy to convince ourselves that we are honest because we live up to the actual words of our promise. But more importantly, we must live up to the intent. Whether it be in sales or any other area of life or business, credibility is our most important asset. It is hard won and easily lost. Our word must not only be golden, but be 24 karat.

This little light of mine, I'm gonna let it shine.
Hymn

HOW DEEP IS BEAUTY?

How many times have we heard someone say, "Beauty is only skin deep." In my experience, it is usually said by one who has been blessed with physical beauty to make someone not so blessed feel better. Even though I have heard the statement many times, I've never given it a lot of thought. If you had asked me if I agreed with it, I probably would have said, "Yes." But now, I feel quite certain that it's not complete. The following incident caused me to change my mind.

I met a young woman who was very attractive, and I found that she had worked with young people. During our discussion, the question of how teenagers view themselves arose. She pointed out that the teenage years are the most critical in developing lifelong self–esteem, and that those who were not blessed with physical attractiveness were most in need of positive reinforcement. It was at that point that I made the comment that she had probably told them, "Beauty is only skin deep." After all, she was a very pretty woman, and they're the kind of words that pretty people use to placate plain people. Her reply set me to thinking.

She said that she had made that statement many times, but it wasn't until the doctor told her that she had cancer and would be undergoing both radiation and chemical therapy that she was faced with having to believe her own words. After several months of treatment, she related that her complexion was ashen, her hair had fallen out, her once slim figure had been bloated by 30 pounds of additional weight, and due to an unrelated condition, braces had been put on her teeth.

Now, she had to make the choice whether, in this condition, she would stand up in front of these young people and continue her program. Did she really believe that beauty was only skin deep? Did she believe that true beauty went all the way through? Could she stand the personal embarrassment she felt at the loss of her physical beauty? The answer to each of these questions, she explained, was, "Yes." In the next several months, she continued to work. She found that her young charges took her illness and its side effects in stride.

By example, she proved that physical beauty is only skin deep, but true beauty goes all the way through. Confirmation of this came from one of the girls who wrote a letter telling her that her example spoke more eloquently than any words.

I believe that all of us are like stained glass windows. Sometimes, if the sun hits us right, we have a certain amount of beauty. But the true beauty of any stained glass window comes when the lights are turned on inside the building. This young woman found that when she turned the light on inside, she was even more beautiful than she had been before. Each of us has that option. Don't hesitate to turn the light on and, like her, shine for all to see.

What the mind of man can conceive and believe, he can achieve.

Napoleon Hill

A TWO–EDGED SWORD

The power of belief in human history has always been a two–edged sword. If we believe that something is possible, one of us is bound to begin trying to do it. With that effort always comes the raising of the human race to a new plateau of knowledge. The reverse side of the belief sword is called doubt. When mankind's knowledge is shrouded in doubts about its ability to achieve some goal, there is little chance that it will be accomplished until such time as fate intervenes or someone dares to show the way.

A primary and very graphic example of this premise is the story of Roger Bannister. Roger Bannister, a British athlete, was an exemplary runner. His forte' was the mile. Until May 6, 1954, he believed, as did all of the rest of the civilized world, that a person could not run a mile in less than four minutes. To that time, no one had run a mile in less than four minutes and there was much medical "evidence" to support the idea that it was physically impossible. With this as a background, he lined up at the starting line in Oxford, England on May 6, 1954, to compete in the mile run. The gun went off and Bannister stretched his legs and began running a measured race. At about the half–mile mark, he heard footsteps close behind him and began to pick up the pace. The faster he ran, the closer the footsteps sounded and the more he was prompted to run faster and faster. When he crossed the finish line, he had set a world's record, and there was no one even close to him. He crossed the finish line at 3 minutes 59.4 seconds. The noise that he had heard, which sounded like footsteps, was actually the number that he wore on his back which had broken loose and flapped as he ran.

Roger Bannister had not only defeated the four-minute mile, but more importantly, he had defeated the doubt which plagued all of humanity since the beginning of time. He had taken an artificial limit and destroyed it. He set the tone for what others could believe, and in the year following his breaking the four-minute mile, eleven more runners equaled or bettered his time. The difference can only be that they now believed that the four-minute mile could be broken. The legacy of this has been a continual improvement in the running of a mile until Steve Cram of the United Kingdom ran it in 3 minutes 46.32 seconds at Oslo in July 1985.

The power of belief in our lives is, indeed, a two-edged sword. If we believe we are incapable of something, we probably will not even try to accomplish it. Few of us will be as lucky as Roger Bannister—to have some thing or some one encourage us or push us to new heights. The answer, then, lies in not deciding that something cannot be done until we make an honest effort to do it.

Winning isn't everything, but the will to win is.
Vince Lombardi

I'D RATHER WATCH A WINNER

I've always thought a person's actions were an indication of whether their word was gold or if it would turn green with time. There are many in our world who talk a good game, but when you watch them, you find out talk is their major product. Recently, I found a poem that says better than I had ever seen before how I feel about words vs. actions. I don't know who wrote it but I'd love to shake his/her hand, because I do believe within it there is great truth.

I'd rather watch a winner, than hear one any day,
I'd rather have one walk with me than merely show the way.
The eye's a better pupil and more willing than the ear;
Fine counsel is confusing, but example's always clear.
And the best of all the coaches are the ones who live their creed;
For to see the good in action is what everybody needs.
I can soon learn how to do it if you'll let me see it done;
I can watch your hands in action, but your tongue too fast may run.
And the lectures you deliver may be very wise and true;

But I'd rather get my lessons by observing what you do.

For I may misunderstand you and the high advice you give;

But there's no misunderstanding how you act and how you live. I'd rather watch a winner, than hear one any day!

The truly successful people, the winners and leaders in life, are those who not only talk a good game but, more importantly, play a good game. They are the coaches who maintain themselves in good physical condition so that when they walk on the field the young people that they coach have a model to follow, not just hollow words. They are the Good Samaritans of life who do not talk about love and caring but rather act upon it in their daily lives. They are the men and women who run their businesses so as to make a profit and yet in a manner that makes society better. They are the people who know duty as a personal thing. Mother Teresa said, "Duty comes from knowing the need to take action and not just the need to urge others to do something." True leaders know that leadership by definition requires that they be out in front showing the way.

Henry David Thoreau once made the statement, "Your actions speak so loudly that I cannot hear what you are saying." If that same statement were applied to your life, what do you think those around you are seeing? Would they say of you, "I'm watching a winner"? I hope so!

*People should be honored for the warmth of
their doors, not the strength of their walls.*

W. N. Hodges

BETTER THAN MEDICINE

Whenever I write a column about hugging, I take a
round of good natured flack from many of my
friends. Be that as it may, let me once again try to
explain why I feel the lowly hug is so important in
our lives.

While doing a program for the staff of a nursing
home, there was a minor interruption when one of
the residents entered the room. The director of the
nursing home immediately asked the old gentleman
to please leave. He felt that if the residents were
allowed to come in, they might be disruptive. On the
other hand, I felt that they would enjoy the program,
and that if he was willing to let them stay, I certainly
was. Slowly, the room began to fill with the older
folks, and as the director had predicted, occasionally
they did pipe up and make comments as I presented
the material. But none of them were in any way rude
or disruptive.

At the end of the program, the room was very neatly
divided between us and them. The staff sat in a
cluster in the middle of the room, and the residents
sat in chairs arranged around the walls. When I
suggested that everyone stand up and hug, the staff
did as I asked and hugged each other. The residents
remained seated. I walked to the back of the room
and asked one of the residents, an older woman
whose face was scarred with pockmarks, to please

give me a hug. She replied in a very deep voice, "I don't hug." "Why don't you hug?" I asked. She replied, "I'm too ugly, no one ever wanted to hug me." I told her that I needed a hug and would she mind giving me one. Hesitantly, she replied, "I guess I can, if you need one." After giving her a hug, I noticed the little grey haired lady sitting next to her had tears flowing down her face. I asked her why she was crying. In a frail voice, she said, "I didn't get a hug." To make a long story short, I gave each of the residents a hug, and then I told them that since I couldn't be there everyday, if they were to get their hugs, they would have to begin hugging each other.

Two weeks later the director called me and said, "Bill, you won't believe the miracle that has occurred here. We used to have to use medication to help our patients sleep at night, but now every night before they go to bed, they go around and hug each other. As a result, many of them seem to be able to sleep drug-free." I said that that really was a miracle, and he said, "Oh no, Bill, that's not the miracle. The miracle is that every Tuesday we have a doctor who visits our facility and our residents line up down the hall to get to see the doctor. This last Tuesday, he was lonelier than the Maytag repairman. They didn't need him to get the touching and stroking so necessary for good health."

A hug, in itself, may not be a miracle cure, but it certainly beats anything that comes in a bottle. If you don't believe me, try it on your family.

The end must justify the means.

Matthew Prior

"SURROUNDED BY TATTLETALES"

To set the tone for this column, let me tell you a story about a young man that I used to know. He was an extremely bright seven–year–old, and wise well beyond his years. Rarely, if ever, was he caught without an answer. Tommy, however, was continually getting caught. His teacher, in exasperation, kept him after school. She looked at him and said, "Tommy, I don't know what I'm going to do with you. Mary says you pulled her hair, Jimmy says you broke his bike, and the janitor says he caught you riding a skateboard in the hall. What is your problem?" Tommy looked back at her and without missing a beat, said, "Teacher, my problem is that I'm surrounded by a bunch of tattletales."

Tommy, not unlike many people, sees the response to his actions, not as his problem, but rather as a problem with the people responding. He has difficulty seeing the cause and effect relationship between what he does and the public response to that action. He finds it hard to understand why Mary got mad, when he was simply trying to get her attention. He can't understand why Jimmy would blame him because the bike wasn't strong enough to jump over a curb. And how could the janitor object to him riding a skateboard in that well–polished, empty hall (where better to ride it?). You see, Tommy only sees his side of any given incident. He makes no attempt to consider other people's feelings when he does things. He assumes that since he meant no harm, no one should be upset by his actions.

In most instances, Tommy is not a bad person. He tries to do something nice and it results in someone getting mad, as in the instance with Mary. You see, he just wanted Mary to know that he liked her, and the only way he knew to get her attention was to pull on her hair. The fact that he would hurt her in doing it never crossed his mind.

Tommy is not unlike the many thousands of people each day who go blithely about their business without an understanding of the consequences of their actions or the problems that they cause for those around them. They don't mean to cause trouble, and they don't even understand why people respond negatively to them.

If we happen to recognize ourselves as one of these people, it might be well that we begin to review our actions, not only as to their intent, but as to their possible result. If, on the other hand, we are put in the position of having to deal with a Tommy, it is imperative that we let him know how we feel about the incident. And since he probably doesn't understand our reaction, it is important that we let him know why we feel the action was inappropriate.

Rarely do the ends justify the means, and it important for all of us, prior to any action, to understand fully the consequences of and accept responsibility for that action.

Have no friends not equal to yourself.

Confucius

ONE OF THE CROWD

As a young person, I had the opportunity to attend nine different schools in two countries before I graduated from high school. From this experience, I learned many lessons. One of those lessons was that being a part of a crowd was not all that it was cracked up to be.

You see, I found that in order to be a part of the crowd, I had to sell at least some small portion of my own individuality. And as a result, I ceased to act like myself and was forced to emulate the leaders of the group. Being a part of the group did provide ready companionship and, in some instances, status. But the rules of the game said that if I was going to be a part of this group, I certainly could not associate with those who my group deemed either weird or inferior.

For me, this posed an insurmountable dilemma. You see, my grades were good enough to associate with the scholars, but I was also a letterman in athletics, and at that time doing both was not the norm. My scholar friends could not understand why I would hang around with the "jocks" and the athletes could not understand why I would want to associate with the "eggheads." To complicate matters, one of my best friends was a shop student, and the manual arts students didn't associate with either the "eggheads" or the "jocks." In the final analysis, if I was to enjoy the friendships of these varied individuals, I found that I could not choose up sides and "belong" to a crowd. That was one of the best decisions of my life. Over the years, it has paid off innumerable times. Because I did not rely upon the group to give me identity, I found that I already had an identity. I traded the security, and maybe the prestige, of belonging to a particular clique for the lifelong knowledge that I could prosper without having to conform to some artificial group norm.

Being a part of a crowd is easy. Look at any field of sheep—one looking and doing just like the other. In fact, that flock of sheep, once a leader is established, will follow the leader blindly, even to slaughter. Whole nations have become flocks of sheep. In the 1930's, Germany allowed an out–of–work house painter to become the leader of the flock. The people of Germany followed this leader into the slaughter that we have come to know as World War II. In the name of the group, millions of people were put to death and yet, when the trials were held in Nuremberg, the defendants pleaded innocent by reason that they were only carrying out the orders of the group. It was a stiff price to pay in order to belong to that infamous fraternity.

Each of us has a choice. We can be a part of the crowd. We can be a follower, and allow others to make our decisions and set our standards. Or we can retain our independence and be a friend to all who seek our friendship. Remember you are unique, you are special, you are great. Don't hesitate to act that way.

The world is an oyster, but you don't crack it on a mattress.

Arthur Miller

THE PRICE OF THE PRIZE

How many of us would like to quarterback a Big 10 team? How many of us would like to win seven gold medals in the Olympics, then be paid $10,000 for shaving off our moustaches on television?

How many of us are willing to throw 500 footballs a day for six years as OSU's Art Schleister did? That was the price he paid for his prize—to quarterback a Big 10 team.

Can you imagine spending 17,000 hours in the water swimming? Mark Spitz did. That is the equivalent of 2,125 working days in the water (without coffee breaks). That was the price he paid for the prize he sought.

You say that it's not fair to ask you to compare yourself to people like Spitz and Schleister who have exemplary athletic talents. Not too long ago, at a local Olympics, I saw a young girl, a special young girl, but she didn't look like an athlete. She had none of the overt characteristics. Her arms hung at strange angles to her body, her feet moved with great effort, but the 25 yards she ran were the most exciting of my life. I hurt for her every step of the way. She crossed the line in almost sheer exhaustion to receive her prize—a simple ribbon and a small medal. The look in this special young woman's eyes told the story. She had beaten no one for she was the only one in the race, yet she had mastered herself and captured the hearts of all of us at the Special Olympics. The prize to her was worth the price.

A great leader once said, "I have a dream." Each of us has a dream, something we want to be when we grow up, maybe even something we've never shared with another human being. It may be something of great magnitude or some small promise that we made to ourselves years ago. It is not until we activate this dream and make it a reality that we begin to pursue our prize in earnest. Today, will you join with me in taking that dream off the shelf, dusting it off, and polishing it up? Will you commit to the thought that you would rather try something great and fail, than do nothing and succeed? Tonight, would you take one more step toward your dream? Before you go to bed, write down your prize and then list the price you will have to pay. If it is worth it, get started.

Shakespeare said, "The fault, dear Brutus, lies not in our stars but in ourselves." Today, we can safely paraphrase that to: Success, dear friends lies, not in our stars but in ourselves and in our willingness to pay the price of the prize.

The best mirror is an old friend.

George Herbert

DISTORTED IMAGES

Once upon a time, there was a king who had such a poor self–image that he didn't want to see himself, so he sent out a royal decree demanding that all mirrors in the kingdom be destroyed. The princess in this kingdom was a beautiful child and yet had never had the opportunity to see herself. One day, while walking, she came upon a group of people beside a placid pond. When she saw the water, she felt joy in her heart in anticipation of finally being able to see her reflection. As she neared the water, the people began throwing stones into the pond. They shouted names at her because they were un-happy with her father's edict, and the stones caused ripples in the water that distorted her reflection. Try as she might, all she could see in the water was this distorted and ugly representation of who she was.

Many of us have much in common with the princess. You see, we may not look into mirrors or ponds to see who we are, but we are always searching for our reflection in the eyes and actions of others. This reflection can be distorted by the stones thrown (in the form of words) by the persons to whom we are looking for validation. The more respect that we have for them, the more damaging their stones can be. An example of this might be a respected super-visor, who in the heat of the moment or because of transitory pressures, berates an employee by calling him/her dumb or stupid. Because the employee respects the supervisor's opinion, he/she begins to accept the dumb or stupid label. As a result, the employee begins to feel incapable and the work slips even further which may bring on a repeat of the supervisor's negative comments. This can become a never–ending cycle until the employee's self–image is totally destroyed.

There is an old song which says, "You always hurt the ones you love—the ones you shouldn't hurt at all." And yet, in the guise of love and caring, we have a tendency to tell people, especially those who we love, many negative things for their own good. However, I have yet to have someone start a sentence with, "I think you ought to know this for your own good . . ." then proceed to praise one of my positive characteristics. Almost always, a statement starting in this manner will be a rock in my pond and a distortion of my self–image.

The princess was smart enough not to accept the image created by the rocks thrown in the first pond as a true picture of who she was. We, like the princess, must also continue to search until we can surround ourselves with people who will help us to find calm waters in order that we can see our true beauty. We must avoid people who tear us down by concentrating on our deficiencies, and we must seek out those people who will build us up by concentrating on our strengths. Remember, you are unique, you are great, and you are special. See yourself that way.

A community is like a ship; everyone ought to be prepared to take the helm.

Henrik Ibsen

FROM THE WHITE HOUSE TO OUR HOUSE

In an interview, Mr. Robert Woodson, president of the National Center for Neighborhood Enterprises, was asked what he thought about our national government. He replied that there is a great deal of preoccupation on the part of the average voter with what is happening in Washington, DC. He went on to say, "It's not the decisions made in the White House, but those made in your house that count." He pointed out that if we are truly to have an impact on the political process and regain control of our own lives, we can have the greatest return on our effort by becoming active at the local level.

Think to yourself, in the city in which you live, how many of your city councilpersons can you call by name? Can you put a face to them? How many of your county officials do you know? If you label yourself with a party designation, such as Republican or Democrat, can you name the county chairman of your party, or any of the precinct captains? Don't feel bad if you don't know the answers. Surveys have shown that less than 10 percent of the American public could answer all of these questions. As a result, we are unfamiliar with those who administer our government.

Walter Lippman made the statement, "In a free society, the state does not administer the affairs of men. It administers justice among men who conduct their own affairs." The key words are "conduct their own affairs." In order to do that, we must take an active interest, not only in the flash and glitter of national politics but, more importantly, in those politicians who are directly within our reach. Do not hesitate to make appointments with the candidates to find out what they stand for. Demand that they give you concrete answers to your questions. It is not reasonable to expect that they will have all the answers or that they will agree with you on all points. After a conscientious review of all the candidates, make a decision to support one or more to the extent that you are able. Support can be in the form of making a financial contribution, addressing envelopes, or simply allowing the candidate to place a sign in your yard.

It is easy for each of us to say, "I'm too busy," or "You can't fight city hall," and then sit back and do nothing. But when you do nothing, do not be surprised when you get equivalent value in return. If Lippman is right, it is imperative that we elect the most qualified people so that we get the best justice, and that we start this process where it will affect us the most—not at the White House but right here at home.

People ask for criticism, but they want only praise.

W. Somerset Maugham

SHAPING OUR WORLD

Somerset Maugham is quoted as saying, "There's a common idea that success spoils people by making them vain and egotistical." Do you agree with this statement? Has this been your experience? I hope not, for Maugham went on to say, "but actually this is erroneous. On the contrary, success makes people—for the most part—humble, tolerant, and gentle. It is failure that makes people bitter and cruel."

If Maugham is correct, and I believe him to be, can you imagine what a great world this would be if everyone considered themselves successful—a whole world of humble, tolerant, and gentle people—humble, not self–effacing; tolerant, not just long suffering; and gentle, not meek.

A world like this could be created if each of us would take time out of our busy schedule to make all of those around us feel needed and important. It is not the big things we do with other people that cause them to gain self–esteem, but rather the small things. It is taking the time to praise a child for being able to tie his or her own shoes, or learning to use the potty. It is giving lavish praise for each newly learned capability. It is looking at a picture that your child has drawn and saying, "That's great." rather than, "Skies aren't purple; they're blue. Trees are green, not yellow." Remember, Picasso made millions of dollars painting purple trees and orange cows. Helping to build success traits in others involves paying sincere compliments. When your friend, Roy, who rarely dresses up, goes to the trouble of wearing a tie, tell him he looks nice, not, "You clean up well." Back–handed compliments do nothing to build a success pattern. They may even cause the person to be self–conscious and not to make the effort again. On the other hand, positive comments invariably build a success feeling in the person to whom you are speaking. They tend to build positive habits through positive reinforcement. Our world, as it relates to people, is fragile because it is made up of many different types of people with many unique needs. It is very easy to destroy, with an offhand comment said in jest or exasperation, any sense of success that they might have felt. On the other hand, if we use praise, admiration, and encouragement with each person we meet, we begin to build a pattern of success for them.

It is really up to us whether we build this world on the precepts of success or we allow it to slip into the abyss of failure. Whatever we choose, we are in it together. We have a vested interest in the success of others, for they will help to shape our world.

Yard by yard, life is hard. Inch by Inch, life's a cinch.

Robert Schuller

GAINING CONTROL OF YOUR LIFE

One of the most difficult battles that we all face is the battle to control our own lives. In order to win this battle, we must overcome those forces both external and internal, which shake our confidence. No battle is without some pain, and no great purpose has ever been accomplished without effort. So it is with this struggle, but we can win.

First, we must control the workings of our own minds and not allow others to do our thinking. Each of us is endowed with a conscience that, if we listen to it carefully, will guide us in the right direction. Begin to believe and trust in yourself.

Another approach to controlling your own life is to be busy without interfering with the lives of others. No life can be in control that is not in harmony, and so it is extremely important that we do everything possible to use our efforts to establish harmony in our work, social, and home environments. However, this does not mean that we should give in to the unreasonable requests of others, but rather that we endeavor to use our talents to the best advantage for both ourselves and those around us.

Being realistic in what you expect of life is another important aspect of gaining control over your destiny. Unfortunately, many people, when they tell you to be realistic, are telling you to settle for less than what you can really achieve. Few would have thought it realistic to expect that someone, who at the age of two had lost both her sight and her hearing, could rise to international prominence as both an author and a lecturer. In fact, most of the world agreed that it was not realistic. Yet, because of the love, patience, and true understanding of the word "realistic," her friend, confidant, tutor, and nurse, Anne Sullivan, drew this little girl, Helen Keller, out of the abyss of darkness that surrounded her and brought her into a world of true reality. You see, Anne Sullivan saw reality as possibilities. She saw that taking control of her own life meant developing her own powers to the extent that she could positively impact those around her.

Dr. Robert Schuller made the statement, "Yard by yard, life is hard. Inch by inch, life's a cinch." Be careful in your endeavor to take control of your life that you don't try to bite off too big a chunk at once. Small successes added one upon another are like the blocks that built the great pyramids. One by one, they had little significance, but combined, they became one of the seven wonders of the world. You, too, can be a wonder if, with patience, you'll pile the success blocks up one by one.

Whatever is worth doing at all is worth doing well.

Philip Dormore Stanhope

PROFESSIONALISM

When most of us hear that a person is a "professional," we have the normal tendency to jump to the conclusion that that person is involved in the practice of such elite professions as teaching, law, medicine, accounting, or other such revered pursuits. It is reasonable for us to jump to this conclusion, since one of Webster's principal definitions of "professional" is: one engaged in one of the learned professions.

I believe that professionals go well beyond this definition. They come in all occupations. They provide a multitude of services, many of which would bring society to a standstill if they were not performed, and when these services are performed poorly, they remove a great deal of joy from life. One of the most professional people that I have ever met was an airport limousine driver. His route was from the Columbus Airport to downtown Columbus, stopping at each of the hotels and then returning to the airport. The job was tedious, the traffic was horrendous, and the trips were numerous. But this man was a professional. His limousine was clean. He always met you with a friendly greeting. Your luggage was handled with care, and as we traveled into the city, he made it a point to explain the sights we were seeing. Although Columbus is a beautiful city, the route from the airport travels through some blighted areas. This man, rather than pointing out the dilapidated buildings, pointed out that this part of Columbus was important in the anti–slavery, underground railway. And, instead of seeing old buildings that were crumbling, he helped us to see a struggle for freedom. He did not see himself simply as a limousine driver, but as an ambassador for the city of Columbus.

This man is just one example of the many people who I consider to be true professionals. I remember one of my secretaries who on a rush project found a minor error in a letter. In my hurry to send it out, I made the mistake of saying, "It is good enough." She then pointed out to me that when the letter was received the reader would think, "What a stupid secretary he must have," and it wasn't good enough for her. She was a professional. Last week, in a neighboring city, as I drove down the road, I noticed that on one street the garbage cans had been emptied very sloppily. The empty cans laid on their sides and there was trash that had spilled from the cans. Further down the block, I noticed another crew picking up garbage. This crew was making it a point to pick up things that had fallen from the cans and to place the cans upright with their lids on. These men were professionals. They cared.

In my mind, professionalism has nothing to do with academic degrees, it's doing the best job you know how to and treating everyone with respect. Are you a professional?

The real leader has no need to lead, he is content to point the way.

Henry Miller

AN EMPLOYEE'S VIEW OF A GOOD BOSS

Over the past five years, I have been asking the attendees in my seminars to write down the three most important attributes that they feel must be present in a good boss. I don't think the following results will surprise you, but sometimes it's good to remind ourselves of what others expect of us when we find ourselves in a position of leadership. The top ten responses to what a good boss should do or be are as follows:

1. A good boss must be a good listener. Many employees feel very frustrated because they do not perceive that their boss is paying attention to what they have to say.

2. A good boss is one who is a leader rather than a shover. A good boss shows the way by action, not just words.

3. A good boss is one who is supportive in times of difficulty and demonstrates that loyalty is the mortar that holds any team together.

4. A good boss is one who, when he or she receives credit for a good idea that was submitted by an employee, is secure enough to credit the employee with the idea.

5. A good boss is a clock watcher, in a positive sense, and notices when employees put in extra effort and then compensates the employee for this devotion to duty.

6. A good boss is one who attempts to be fair, and, before making a decision, will listen to all sides of a dispute.

7. A good boss is one who is consistent, yet flexible. Employees are given guidelines for their actions, but they are allowed to use creativity in performing their duties.

8. A good boss is one who provides employees with challenges, growth, and promotion opportunities.

9. A good boss is one who praises in public and criticizes in private.

10. A good boss is one who truly cares about his or her employees.

The attributes above are not ranked in a particular order, however, number 10 was the most often mentioned. In my estimation, if you are a success at number 10, the other nine will take care of themselves.

If passion drives, let reason hold the reins.
Benjamin Franklin

LOOK WHO MADE THE TOP TEN STRESS LIST!

Much has been written about high–stress jobs. When we think of stressful occupations, we think of police officers, surgeons, air traffic controllers, and airline pilots. A report just released by the National Institute on Workers' Compensation; American Institute of Stress, on the top ten tough jobs in America listed within it two occupations which I was initially surprised to see included. These two professions are waitress and secretary. Upon further thought, it became clear why these two professions made the high–stress category. Each has a high degree of responsibility and yet, for the most part, a very low degree of authority. Many a boss is prone to tell a secretary to get a job done but doesn't give the authority to commit the resources necessary to accomplish the project. The waitress takes the flack for everything from a late reservation to the chef overcooking a prime rib. Neither the waitress nor the secretary has the appropriate authority to match their responsibility and,as a result, anger builds, culminating in stress.

Does your job fall into this responsibility without authority category?

So many jobs do that stress is rampant in America. We can protect ourselves by recognizing the warning signs of stress overload. Some of the warning signs are frequent illnesses, such as headaches and colds; insomnia, even though one seems to be suffering from persistent fatigue; irritability, displayed through overreaction to minor incidents; and most importantly, increased use of alcohol and drugs.

In order to cope with our stressful society, we must do everything possible to keep ourselves in good physical condition. The business stress that causes us to be lethargic and yet prevents us from sleeping can be overcome by a regimen of reasonable exercise. Something as simple as having your partner give you a rubdown with a good body lotion can relieve a lot of tension. (That is, of course, as long as you reciprocate.) Limited alcohol consumtion and a sensible diet can reduce stress levels. Once, the three–martini lunch was an acceptable business practice, and there may have been some excuse for being a part of it; but in today's business world, many lunches have NO martinis and the diet plates outnumber the prime ribs.

Each of the above suggestions will help reduce stress, but stress caused by being in a position of responsibility without authority can only be corrected by the employer, and only if you have the courage to make your feelings known. This may not be easy, but remember, without your health, many things will not be easy. As a final resort, the two most important things in controlling stress are understanding what you have control of and what you don't, and more importantly, maintaining a good sense of humor.

To conquer without risk is to triumph without glory.

Pierre Corneille

THE RISK–FREE SOCIETY

I watched with interest on the C–Span channel of Cable TV while two senators made a very strong plea for some social legislation that was designed to remove another risk factor from our daily lives. These were good men who, I feel certain, had the best interests of our people at heart. They seemed to truly believe that if they could establish a risk–free society, they would have a perfect America. Their arguments for their way of thinking seemed appealing until another senator rose to speak against the legislation. This senator began to point out that for every risk removed, a right is forfeited. He went on to say that it was people willing to accept risks who built this country, and it is those who are still willing to take risks who continue to cause it to be great.

Each of us has to make the decision whether we wish to live in a country that provides "cradle–to–grave security," or whether we want to reserve the right to accept challenge with the possibility of loss. I believe the following poem, written by an anonymous poet, has much for us to think about. It is entitled "Risk."

> To laugh is to risk appearing the fool
> To weep is to risk appearing sentimental
> To reach out for another is to risk involvement

To expose feelings is to risk exposing your true self

To play your ideas, your dreams before the crowd is to risk their loss

To love is to risk not being loved in return

To live is to risk dying

To hope is to risk despair

To try is to risk failure

But risk must be taken, because the greatest hazard in life is to risk nothing

The person who risks nothing, does nothing, has nothing, and is nothing

He may avoid suffering and sorrow, but he simply cannot learn, feel, change, grow, love

Chained by his certitudes, he is a slave

He has forfeited freedom

Only a person who risks—is free

The freedom to try—to risk—is one of the most cherished rights, of all mankind. We must continually fight to maintain a balance between that which is good for us as a whole, and that which infringes upon the rights of us as individuals. Security without freedom is not security, but rather captivity. Remember the final words of the poem. "Only a person who risks—is free." How free are you?

We are not permitted to choose the frame of our destiny. But what we put into it is ours.
Dag Hammerskjold

THE GARDEN OF LIFE

How does your garden grow? Your answer to this, as it is applied to your life, will depend upon a number of things. A well–ordered, abundant, and bountiful life depends upon the same actions that are required to have an abundant and bountiful garden.

Our lives parallel a garden in many ways, especially in that they follow cycles. It would be ludicrous to assume that if we dug up the ground once, and planted seeds once, that we could expect an abundant crop to appear each year. We all know that for a garden to remain abundant, it must have constant tending. So it is with life!

In the winter, when the ground is frozen and the ability to work the soil is withdrawn from us, we must use that time to search the seed catalogues, to read up on the new planting techniques. In life there are times when, because of temporary setbacks, we are unable to pursue our goal actively. This is the time when we must invest in ourselves by reading and studying the new technology in our field or make the decision to try something new.

In the spring, we plant the seeds (ideas) that we found during the winter. As the tiny shoots begin to grow, our garden is attacked by everything from snails to groundhogs. In the beginning, we planted few seeds and jealously guarded each plant. We have since found that it's easier to plant an abundance of seeds thus allowing for the loss of individual plants. In life, as in our gardens, the more ideas (seeds) we plant, the more likely some of these ideas will survive and bear fruit.

In the summer, the plants must be nurtured by watering, fertilizing, and weeding. In life, ideas too must be nurtured. We must weed out the negative influences, apply the fertilizer of enthusiasm, and soak it in with a cloudburst of faith.

Finally, and maybe most importantly, comes the fall. The fall is when we reap our harvest and prepare the soil for the next growing season. It is a time that we till back into the soil some of what it has given to us. In life, it is also a time when we plow back into our community—through the use of our time, talents, and money—some of the bounty of our harvest.

Life, like a garden, is a never–ending process. If we expect it to continue to bear abundant fruit, we must do our studies, plant wisely and generously, tend it carefully, and be willing to return part of its bounty to whence it came.

Leadership appears to be the art of getting others to want to do something you are convinced should be done.

Vance Packard

THE CARROT AND/OR THE STICK

Motivation, whether used on animals or humans, can take many forms. An old farmer had a mule that was so obstinate that he just couldn't get it to move, even when he hit it with a stick. Finally, he thought he would teach it a lesson, and he built a fire under the mule. Now, the mule was not about to stand there and be roasted. What the mule did was move forward just far enough that the fire was under the farmer's wagon, which promptly burned to the ground.

Motivation by fear can be effective. There is a tale told about a fellow who, having had too much to drink, decided to take a shortcut through a graveyard on his way home. As luck would have it, in his inebriated state, he did not notice an open grave and he fell into it. When he recovered from his initial shock, he began trying to crawl up the sides of the pit in order to escape. Try as he might, he could not get a handhold sufficient to pull himself out of the grave. Finally, resigned to the fact that he would have to stay there, he huddled down in one corner of the grave to await morning. Later that night, another drunk came through the same graveyard and fell into the same grave. He did not notice that the grave was already occupied by his fellow drunk. The second occupant began clawing at the dirt in order to get out, and the din woke up the first gentlemen. Upon waking, the first occupant spoke the words, "You'll never get out!" But HE DID! I expect that a voice from a grave would motivate most of us to extraordinary action. Fear, however, is only a short–term motivator, and lasts only as long as the victim perceives a clear and present danger.

In a recent classroom session, I demonstrated this point by suggesting to the class that if I had a bullwhip and began snapping it at the class, that I could drive them, not only out of the room but out of the building and into the parking lot. One rather bright lady quickly challenged my statement and said that I might be able to drive the class out of the room, but when they walked through the door, they could go either way in the hallway and I would have to make a choice which group I was going to drive, and at each split in the hallway, my whip would lose power. We decided that, at best, I could drive no more than one person all the way to the parking lot with the use of a whip. I then asked how many would meet me in the parking lot if I offered $100 to each person who showed up there by the time I reached the lot. Every hand went up. Motivation by fear is effective only when people have restricted choices. The far better alternative is to motivate by creating an atmosphere where people want to participate.

In motivating, the only role a stick should play is to hold the carrot.

Those who cannot remember the past are con-demned to repeat it.

George Santayana

THE BIRTHDAY PARTY

Think back across your life. How many of the "good times" that you remember were perceived by you to be "tough times" when they happened? One of the good times that I remember came when I was a child, living in a small town in Canada. The year was 1948, the economy was poor, and my family was broke. You'll note that I said the economy was poor, not that my family was poor. I could not remember a time, regardless of how little we had, that we thought of ourselves as poor. Poor is a state of mind that generally becomes a permanent way of life, but broke is temporary. It was my eighth birthday and my mother had the sad duty of telling me that there was no money for a birthday party. Looking back, I know how much that must have hurt both Mom and Dad. Mom did find in the kitchen enough ingredients to make a single layer cake and a can of pineapple.

It wasn't long after that pineapple upside–down cake came out of the oven that we heard a rap at the door. When my dad opened it, there stood three of my little friends.

They acknowledged the fact that there was not a birthday party but they did not want to let the day go by without doing something. They had each brought something of their own to give me as a birthday present. The first brought me a slingshot that he had made with his own hands, and I knew it was one of his prized possessions. The second brought me two used comic books. (Comic books in our neighborhood were a medium of trade, and hence were very valuable.) The last brought me a Cadbury's candy bar, the money for which he had earned sweeping out his Dad's store.

Forty years have passed since that birthday, but I can still see in my mind those three young friends standing in our doorway.

Over the years, I've had many birthday parties, received some very beautiful gifts, and yet none pleased me more than those I received in 1948. You see, what my friends gave me were truly gifts of love. They had so little and yet they were willing to share it with me.

Some have said, "It's not the gift, but the thought that counts." But I believe that it is more likely a combination of the giver's ability to give, the meaning of the gift to the giver, and how much of the giver's self is put into it.

From that birthday on, I have requested a pineapple upside–down cake for my birthday cake. You see, it reminds me of times that were tough, but also of times when love was strong. It reminds me of how far we've come and how important friends are.

Things turn out best for the people who make the best of the way things turn out.

John Wooden

OH, GOD, FORGIVE ME WHEN I WHINE

It was a dark and rainy night. At least that's how Snoopy would start this story. Well, it might not have been dark and rainy, but for several months I had lived with a dull pain in the middle of my back and it then began to radiate down my left leg. As the pain became more intense, I began to say to myself, "Why me, Lord? What have I done?" On thinking about that statement, I quickly added the word "lately." Slowly, as the pain increased, I lost the use of my left leg. As we traveled from doctor to doctor I kept saying to myself, and anyone who would listen, "Why me?"

Finally, I was taken to the hospital for back surgery, and as I recovered, I began looking around me. I saw people who would never walk again, people who would have given anything, even with the pain, to be able to take a step. Slowly, a poem crept into my mind. This poem entitled, "The World is Mine," was written by Jess Kenner and given to me by Thomas S. Haggai, president and chairman of IGA and author of the inspirational book, Today. The poem reads like this:

Today upon a bus, I saw a lovely maid with golden hair. I envied her—she seemed so gay—and wished I were as fair. When suddenly she rose to leave, I saw her hobble down the aisle; she had one foot and wore a crutch, but as she passed, a smile. Oh, God, forgive me when I whine; I have two feet—the world is mine.

And then I stopped to buy some sweets. The lad who sold them had such charm. I talked to him—he said to me, "It's nice to talk to folks like you. You see," he said, "I'm blind." Oh, God, forgive me when I whine; I have two eyes—the world is mine.

Then walking down the street, I saw a child with eyes of blue. He stood and watched the others play; it seemed he knew not what to do. I stopped a moment, then I said, "Why don't you join the others, dear?" He looked ahead without a word, and then I knew, he could not hear.

Oh, God, forgive me when I whine; I have two ears—the world is mine. With feet to take me where I'd go, with eyes to see the sunset glow, with ears to hear what I would know, Oh, God, forgive me when I whine; I'm blessed indeed. The world is mine.

As I reflected upon these words I began to stop asking, "Why me?" and dwelled upon what I did have rather than what I did not have. Maybe it was God's way of showing me how lucky I am—lucky to have such a good wife, family, friends, and people who care. There is no question that in the days ahead I will walk strongly again because of the love of these people. There is no question that I am blessed indeed. The world is mine when I count my blessings rather than whine.

ORDERING INFORMATION

Who do you know who would benefit from reading and owning this book?

- a valued friend
- a recent graduate
- a retiree
- a business associate
- an employee
- your supervisor
- your children
- your parents
- your customers
- a member of your church
- someone in the hospital

Any of the above would be pleased to have a copy and, more importantly, they would appreciate you for giving it to them. If your bookstore will not order it for you, you may order it directly from HODGES SEMINARS.

The price per copy is $4.95.

Shipping & handling $1.25 first copy, 25¢ each additional copy. Ohio residents add 6% sales tax.

Make check payable to Hodges Seminars and send it along with your printed name & address to:

HODGES SEMINARS

P.O. BOX 22, FAIRBORN, OHIO 45324

When you're fanny deep in alligators, it's hard to remember that your primary mission was to drain the swamp.

"Tip Toe Thru The Alligators"

As a dynamic keynote, an after dinner treat, or a great half day "team building" seminar, it will please and inform your audience.

WHAT'S AN ALLIGATOR?

We've all heard the saying, "When you're fanny deep in alligators, it's hard to remember that your primary mission was to drain the swamp." How many of us know who the "alligators" of our lives really are? We're surrounded by many types of people as we do our jobs. Some of them are "alligators"—personality types who can threaten our associates' or our own job performance. In fact, we may be an "alligator" ourselves, or at least exhibit some of the characteristics of one. Alligators are not bad people; they just need help.

Bill Hodges' "TIP TOE THRU THE AL-LIGATORS" allows us to take a nonthreatening look at some of the alligators we're most likely to encounter. Bill uses a unique style of presentation that gives his serious message a light, entertaining flair.

But more important, you'll remember. Bill's use of humor, visual aids, and audience participation serve to reinforce his strong vocal delivery and give you mental pegs upon which to hang his basic points.

This program is designed to help people at all levels deal more effectively with others and themselves. By providing insights to help you overcome some of the basic obstacles to better productivity, harmonious daily interfacing with each other, and positive work attitudes, "TIP TOE THRU THE ALLIGATORS" can help you and your organization increase profits, reduce grievances, and raise productivity.

For more information, call Bill Hodges at 513-878-9701